15869

D0429433

A VIEW FROM THE ZOO

I began my career with the zoo in 1967. It was a golden time. It will never be like that in the zoo world again. It's because the earth is smaller now and the numbers of animals have declined.

The Los Angeles Zoo was the only zoo in history to begin as a major zoo. We saw rare and endangered animals being brought to us in a steady, magnificent stream. The experience was a hands-on gathering unprecedented since the time of Noah, a great adventure.

It is with great joy that I share my best stories with you in hopes of honoring the One who allowed me my golden time, the One who fashioned the animals about which I have written. Come with me now and meet my larger-than-life experience. And laugh a little. This isn't just my view from the zoo . . . it's for all of us. As you turn the pages you will see that life itself is a zoo!

Gary Richmond

Gary Richmond

A
VIEW
FROM THE
ZOO

WORD BOOKS
PUBLISHER
WACO, TEXAS
A DIVISION OF
WORD, INCORPORATED

A VIEW FROM THE ZOO
Copyright © 1987 by Gary Richmond

Unless otherwise indicated, Scripture quotations are from The Revised Stand-
ard Version of the Bible (RSV), copyrighted 1946, 1952, © 1971, 1973 by the
Division of Christian Education of the National Council of the Churches of
Christ in the U.S.A., and used by permission.

Photographs in this publication are by Dale Thompson, George & Kathy
Dodge, and Gary Richmond.

Library of Congress Cataloging-in-Publication Data:

Richmond, Gary, 1944–
 A view from the zoo.

 1. Zoo animals—Miscellanea. 2. Animals—
Miscellanea. 3. Christian life—1960–
I. Title.
QL77.5.R525 1987   242   87–10593
ISBN 0-8499-0632-6
ISBN 0-8499-3084-7 (pbk.)

Printed in the United States of America

This edition has been produced for members of Family Bookshelf and is re-
printed by arrangement with WORD BOOKS, Waco, Texas.

To George and Marcy Burch
Parents, Mentors, and Friends

Contents

Foreword I

Nobody can resist a good story. Maybe it is part of what it means to be created in God's image. The rabbis used to say, "God made people because He loves stories." If that's not completely true about humans, I'm willing to bet it's true about the rest of the animal kingdom . . . kudus, hippos, giraffes, rhinos, and chimpanzees, to name just a few.

Nobody I've ever known can resist one of Gary Richmond's zoo stories. I've seen Gary absolutely enchant a campfire circle of third-graders with his black widow tale one minute, then turn around and do the same with several hundred adults in a conference center auditorium. Flannery O'Connor wrote that "the ability to create life with words is essentially a gift. If you have it in the first place, you can develop it; if you don't have it, you might as well forget it." Gary Richmond definitely has the gift.

The stories you will read in this book have been developed over the last twenty-five years from Gary's unique double-career as a zookeeper and a pastor. While the two jobs are often more similar than might be imagined, they're rarely shared by the same person. Gary has spun his adventures from these two worlds into some of the best yarns you've read in a long time. Not only did they all really happen, each story contains a piece of God's truth told in a way you'll never forget.

Nobody I can imagine will be able to resist these stories. They amuse, interest, and inform. In fact, I'll bet you can't read just one!

Paul Sailhamer, Senior Associate Pastor
First Evangelical Free Church
Fullerton, California

Foreword II

Gary Richmond and I have known each other for years. I was drawn to him long before he became a member of our pastoral team at the First Evangelical Free Church of Fullerton, California.

He is an absolute joy to be around: genuine charisma, quick wit, a zest for life, and always a story or two to add flavor to the moment. His years at the Los Angeles Zoo have given him an enormous depth of appreciation for the animal world. His even greater number of years in vocational Christian service have given him a breadth of understanding of people like you and me. In my opinion, his ability to use the former to illustrate the latter is unparalleled. I know of no one better qualified to communicate truth for today from this unique perspective than Gary.

In addition to being a splendid storyteller and one with a keen awareness of human nature, the man is a fine husband, a devoted father, and a dear friend. I am pleased he accepted the challenge to put his wealth of unusual experiences into print. More than merely "a view from the zoo," these pages contain one mirror after another reflecting images of and insights into ourselves. I suggest, therefore, that you not hurry through these pages. Walk slowly. Pause thoughtfully. There is much to be gleaned from these creatures God has made through the pen of a man God has gifted.

Chuck Swindoll
Pastor, Radio Teacher, Author

Thank Yous

To my wife Carol and my children, Marci, Wendi, and Gary. I first told these stories to Carol on the days they happened and she loved them. My children have made me tell them over and over to their friends. That made the writing much easier.

Thank you to Paul Sailhamer, who has for the last twenty years been my greatest source of encouragement.

Thank you to Chuck Swindoll for his support and daily encouragement. I would also like to thank Chuck for being even better behind the scenes than he is in the spotlight. He has been a great example throughout this project.

Thank you to Helen Peters. Helen made doing the book more fun. Her experience was invaluable as deadlines approached. She always made me feel like she loved the book.

Thank you to Vickie Knoedler. Vickie is my secretary. Her terrific attitude, kind spirit, and patience, not to mention her skills, made writing a book as easy as it could be.

Thank you to Mindy Anderson. Mindy volunteered to share her recently acquired editing skills to the first draft of this work. I received many compliments for her work.

Thank you to Bob Kraning, Executive Director of Forest Home Christian Conference Center. Bob has allowed me to remain Father Nature, a camp naturalist, for the last eighteen summers. It helped me to keep my edge in the nature scene.

Thank you to Dale Thompson, my closest friend, who lived these stories with me. He has also served with me in nature ministries through most of the last eighteen years. His vast knowledge and photographic skills are evident throughout this book.

Thank you to Mike Mace, lead keeper for the birds department at Wild Animal Park. Mike provided an unforgettable day for us at the park and we were able to finish the photography because of it.

Thank you to George and Kathy Dodge for their excellent photographic work. George and I served at the zoo for several years together.

Thank you to Cecile Smith for her work on the earliest phase of the manuscript. She is a good friend, great encouragement, and a fine secretary.

Thank you to Bob Knight for his valued assistance in the preparation of the photographs. He is a special friend.

Thank you to Ernie Owen and Richard Baltzell of Word Books for believing in this venture.

Thank you to Sheri Livingston for her fine editing, her invaluable enhancements of each story, and her great enthusiasm, and to all the people at Word who made a valuable contribution.

Thank you to Bernie and Helen Teunissen for introducing me to Tommy, their white-handed gibbon. Tommy is twenty-six years old, and I thank Tommy for not biting me.

Finally, thank you to Sonny Salsbury, Clarence Zylstra, and Kent Yamaguchi, who have been partners in Mile High Outdoor Education. They have all provided a special influence in my using God's creation as a medium of ministry.

Ten percent of the author's royalties will be given to the ministry of the African Children's Choir. They are presently touring the United States to raise money to house and feed as many of the 150,000 homeless orphans in Uganda as possible. It is a great cause. Help if you can. For more information write:

African Children's Choir
P.O. Box 15209
Seattle, WA 98115

Gary Richmond

Ups and Downs

God has designed thousands of ways for the animal kingdom to come into existence, but in my estimation the birth of the baby giraffe is of all births the most impressive. See it once and you'll never forget it.

The zoo health center was called at 9:30 A.M. and we were informed that the female Angola giraffe was giving birth. If the veterinarian and I wanted to watch we could. Neither of us had ever witnessed a giraffe birth before, so we headed quickly for the giraffe barn. We parked and walked quietly to a location where about seven of us were afforded an earthbound view of an elevated event. I sat on a bale of hay next to Jack Badal, a man considered by most of us to be the greatest animal keeper alive. He was a man of few and well-chosen words, and when I sat down, he only nodded and continued to suck the sweetness from the alfalfa stem he had pulled from the hay bale on which we sat.

I noticed the calf's front hooves and head were already visible and dripping with amniotic fluids. I also noticed that the mother was standing up. "When is she going to lie down?" I said to Jack, who still hadn't said anything.

"She won't," he answered.

"But her hindquarters are nearly ten feet off the ground. That calf might get hurt from the fall," I said. Jack just gave me that look that told me I had probably said something that revealed my ignorance.

I wondered why no plans were being made to procure a fireman's net to catch the baby, so I asked. "Listen, Gary," he said. "You can go try to catch the calf if you want, but remember that its mother has enough strength in her hind legs to kick your head off, which is what she'd do if you get anywhere near that calf. They've killed lions that tried to get their calves."

I was able to sit quietly for a while and observe the calf's journey down the birth canal. Its neck and front legs were fully extended and dangling freely, ten feet above the hard ground on which it was soon to fall. It seemed unbelievable to me that in just a few minutes this newborn was going to be introduced to such trauma. Ten feet! To the hard ground! (It had taken me twelve years to get up the nerve to jump off a high dive approximately ten feet high into clear deep water. This giraffe calf was going to top that during its first thirty minutes of visible existence.)

The moment we had anticipated was not a disappointment. The calf, a plucky male, hurled forth, falling ten feet and landing on his back. Within seconds, he rolled to an upright position with his legs tucked under his body. From this position he considered the world for the first time, shaking some of the last vestiges of birthing fluids from his eyes and ears.

The mother giraffe lowered her head long enough to take a quick look. Then she positioned herself so that she was standing directly over her calf. She waited for about a minute and then did the most unreasonable thing. She swung her pendulous leg outward and kicked her baby, so that it was sent sprawling head over heels (or hooves, in this case). I turned to Jack and exclaimed, "Why'd she do that?"

"She wants it to get up, and if it doesn't she'll do it again."

Jack was right—the violent process was repeated again and then again. The struggle to rise was momentous, and as the baby grew tired of trying, the mother would again stimulate its efforts with a hearty kick.

Finally, amidst the cheers of the animal care staff, the calf stood for the first time. Wobbly, for sure, but it stood. Then we were struck silent when she kicked it off its feet again.

Jack's face was the only face not expressing astonishment. "She wants it to remember how it got up," he offered. "That's why she knocked it down. In the wild it would need to get up as soon as possible to follow the herd. The mother needs the herd, too. Lions, hyenas, leopards, and hunting dogs all would enjoy young giraffes. They'd get it, too, if the mother didn't teach her baby to quickly get up and get with it."

Jack waved good-bye with his alfalfa stem and returned to his section to care for his animals, something he did better than anyone I have ever known.

I've thought about the birth of that giraffe many times since that spring morning and have seen its parallel in my own life. There have been many times when it seemed that I had just stood after a trial only to be knocked down by the next. It was God helping me to remember how it was that I got up, urging me always to walk with Him in His shadow under His care.

Count it all joy, my brethren, when you meet various trials, for you know that the testing of your faith produces steadfastness.

James 1:2–3

Chaca, Uh Uh . . .

The phone rang and my first thoughts were, "Who died?" Why else would anybody call at 12:20 A.M. other than to tell you somebody had died?

"Hello," I answered. This better be really good or really bad, I thought.

"Richmond, how would you like a little adventure in your life?" I recognized the voice of my boss, the zoo's young but very capable veterinarian.

"Sure, what's up?"

"The police just called. They want us to catch a killer ape that's loose in Highland Park. Meet me at the zoo in a few minutes."

As I hung up the phone I found myself wishing he had not said "killer ape." Of course if a killer ape were loose in Highland Park it would need our help. That was a rough neighborhood.

I pushed my car to its limits and the freeway lights and signs charged me like an onslaught of wooden soldiers. They briefly appeared in my rear-view mirror and quickly faded from view. As I drove, I made an inventory of what we might need in the capture of a killer ape. Tranquilizer gun, nets, ropes, and assorted drugs. My damp palms gripped the steering wheel, and I wondered if my boss would notice if I didn't show up. I was probably the only one he called, so I concluded he might.

I skidded around the freeway off-ramp and entered the zoo's immense parking lot. Waiting at the entrance to the zoo was a black and white police car, its red and yellow lights pulsating with anticipation. Two officers were sitting in the front seat.

"Your boss is already at the health center. He wanted us to bring you up." I jumped in the back of the police car and we screamed passed the security guard who was manning the gate. "Killer ape, huh?" I asked.

"Tore up his master real good. Went after one of our officers too. That ape is one mean son of a gun." (The officer didn't exactly say "son of a gun.") "One of our guys discharged his revolver at it, but he missed. We'll get the sucker, though."

By the time we pulled up to the zoo health center, Dr. Bill Hulsizer had already gathered everything we would need. We threw it in their trunk and jumped into the back seat. The car lurched forward, and in no time we were on the freeway with siren howling. We passed several cars, all of which looked as though they were standing still. I glanced at the speedometer and noticed that we were going ninety miles an hour.

I turned towards Bill and asked, "So what do you think we're up against?"

He was the scientific type and would not speculate. He shrugged his shoulders and said, "We'll see."

I have always suffered from an over-active imagination, and it wouldn't have surprised me if King Kong himself stepped on the police car when we got there. We flew down the off-ramp and wove our way deep into a residential area. It looked as though we had entered a war zone. The officers were stopped by a crusty sergeant who pointed into the night and said, "They're waitin' for you at the command post."

"Command post," I said with a tinge of sarcasm in my voice. "What did you get us into, Doctor?"

"We'll see," he said with a wry smile. Boy, sometimes those scientific types can really make you mad.

There were police cars everywhere. All of them had their lights flashing on and off, and all of the neighbors were clustered in small groups, discussing the crisis. We arrived at the command post, and an officer with plenty of authority called for a mass meeting. Officers began showing up from everywhere. I'm sure there were more than fifty. We were brought to the center of the group and the officer with all the authority said, "Men, this is Dr. Bill Hulsizer and his assistant Gary Richmond. These guys are experts from the zoo. They're going to help us track down the ape." He turned to us and said, "You guys are in charge. What do you want us to do?"

Bill and I looked at each other and I think we both wanted to laugh. Bill was the shy type. He was a very competent veterinarian, but there was no way he was going to order around the policemen that surrounded us. I didn't want to usurp his authority so I waited for him to make the first move. He put his arm on my shoulder and said, "Gary is the capture expert. Let's let him take charge."

"Take it," said the man with the biggest badge. So I did.

"Is there anybody here who has actually seen the animal we are after?" I probed.

A young officer stepped forward and said, "I did, sir."

"Can you describe him for us?"

"The light wasn't too hot. He was big, though. I discharged my revolver at him, but I believe I missed. Scared the heck out of me." (The officer didn't exactly say "heck.")

"Is the owner around here or any neighbors who have seen the animal? It would really be helpful if we knew what we were after."

The owner's father was brought to us, and as it turned out, he was the man who had been attacked. Most of his upper body was bandaged, including his face. The owner was in jail on several counts, all having to do with possessing or selling narcotics. It seems that he had developed a drug habit in Vietnam and brought it home with him. That's not all he brought with him. He also brought home a young pet that grew up to be something very large and very dangerous. I asked the man if he had a photograph of his son's pet. He said he did and reached for his wallet. As he handed me the picture he explained how he had sustained his injuries. It seems that while his son was in jail the responsibility of feeding the creature was his. The creature only liked the son, and attempting to get food into the cage was a daily act of courage. This was the night the father lost the battle. Blood was seeping through his gauze bandages, and I could just feel the tension building among the officers. I studied the photograph and was somewhat relieved to discover that the "killer ape" was really just a large monkey. It was a stump-tailed macaque—a very large specimen with two-inch canines.

I addressed the father once more, "Is there anything the monkey likes?" I was thinking of a favorite food item and was unprepared for the man's answer.

He was a Mexican-American gentleman and said with great enthusiasm, "Chaca likes it when you say, 'Chaca, Uh Uh.' I don't know why, but it calms him down." I thanked him very much for his help and began to speak to the assembly of policemen.

"Officers, I have very good news for you. We are not after a killer ape but a very large monkey named Chaca. Chaca is not the kind of animal that you would need to

A VIEW FROM THE ZOO

shoot, and frankly, I will not help you look for him if *I* have to worry about getting shot. If it would make you feel better, carry your night sticks. The owner's father has just told me that their pet likes it when you say, 'Chaca, Uh Uh,' so I suggest that as you go through the neighborhood you repeat that phrase over and over. We will wait here until he is sighted then we will take over. He is most likely scared to death after being shot at and is simply hiding."

As the officers spread out, Dr. Hulsizer leaned over to me and said, "Gary, it's not going to do any good for them to be saying, 'Chaca, Uh Uh.'"

"It will too. It will keep them calm. If they think they're helping their own cause they might not shoot each other." Then Bill and I got the giggles as Los Angeles's finest went from house to house and from garage to garage saying, "Chaca, Uh Uh."

A police helicopter thundered overhead and turned on its blinding searchlight. Backyards were bathed in light, and although it was 2:00 A.M. we had the passing sensation of walking about in broad daylight. Walkie-talkies crackled and squeaked as policemen checked in to report that they had not sighted Chaca. The helicopter search was finally called off, and we again heard the masculine chant, "Chaca, Uh Uh . . . Chaca, Uh Uh." It sounded like a soundtrack from an old jungle movie and it would have fit the moment if someone had said, "The natives are getting restless."

At 2:45 A.M., an officer came running up to us and announced that his partner had Chaca cornered in a garage. We grabbed our equipment and hurried to the site. Most of the policemen were already there. They parted to let us through so that we might enter the side door of the garage. When we got inside, we saw Chaca huddled under a small fishing boat which was sitting snugly on its boat trailer. Chaca was protecting his face from the bright beam of light that issued forth from the sergeant's blue-steel

22

flashlight. Chaca's body language was screaming, "Don't shoot, please don't shoot!"

His capture was not in the least dramatic. We laid a net over his trembling body and he fell over. I believe he was very near to fainting. We transferred Chaca to a travel cage and took him back to the zoo. He was kept there for thirty days in quarantine to determine whether or not he was carrying any transmissible diseases. He was then moved to another facility and we never saw him again.

It was after 4:00 A.M. when I crawled back into bed. It had been a great adventure and one with a happy, injury-free conclusion. It was clearly one of the most memorable experiences of my entire life. I cannot recall any deliberate thought concerning God during the whole night. But He was there, caring, protecting. And I can't prove it but I think He was laughing. One of the most comforting thoughts that I have ever entertained is from a quote by Ruth Harms Calkins from her classic book of poems, *Tell Me Again Lord, I Forget.*

> Loving me as you do,
> You understand so well,
> That when I want you least
> I need you most.*

You see, even when I am not thinking of Him, He is thinking of me. It is then that He comes to me and in my weakness His strength is made perfect.

If you want to get a feel for the depth of this truth then put down this book and read the Book of Esther. It is the only book in the Bible that never mentions God in any way. Nothing supernatural is mentioned. But from the first to the last page God is there, developing the character of a beautiful woman and protecting His people.

*From TELL ME AGAIN, LORD, I FORGET by Ruth Harms Calkin. Published by Tyndale House Publishers, Inc. © 1986. Used by permission.

Be Careful! You Might
Let Out a Bear

I'll never forget the feelings I experienced when two shiny new keys were pressed firmly into my trembling hands. They weren't just any keys. These keys gave me access to all the cages at the Los Angeles Zoo. The supervisor, a crusty veteran, admonished me solemnly concerning the use and care of these keys.

"Richmond," he said, "these keys will let you in to care for millions of dollars worth of animals. Some of them could never be replaced, but you could be, if you catch my drift. Some of the animals would hurt themselves if they got out, and more significantly, they might hurt and even kill somebody. You wouldn't want that on your conscience.

"And, Richmond, don't lose the keys. The big boys in administration don't take it too well if you lose the keys. It works out best if they can't hear your name much until you pass probation six months from now."

The longer we talked the heavier the keys became. I discovered that most of the veterans (five years or more of service) had let out animals. And if I stayed at the zoo, sooner or later it would happen to me. Somehow my job security was tied to how I cared for these keys, and they seemed heavier still.

He gave me several tips on key care, use, and safety, and emphasized the value of getting into a routine. "Consistency is your best safeguard," he said. "Do it the same way at every exhibit. Develop a good habit and don't vary your routine."

I took him seriously and performed flawlessly for four months. I received sterling evaluations for my safety habits—then something happened.

I couldn't tell you why my routine varied, but somehow it did and with the most dangerous animal at the zoo. Ivan was a polar bear who weighed well over nine hundred pounds and had killed two prospective mates. He hated people and never missed an opportunity to attempt to grab anyone passing by his cage. Many of us had experienced nightmares featuring Ivan. And one of the thoughts most discussed among the keepers was the horrifying question, "What if Ivan got out?"

For more than one hundred consecutive workdays I had cared for this nightmare, never coming close to making a mistake. Then I let him out of his night quarters into the sparkling morning sunshine by pulling a lever which lifted a five-hundred-pound steel guillotine door. No sooner had he passed under it than I realized that I had left the steel door that had given me access to the outside exhibit (where he now was) wide open. At any minute he might be walking down the hall and around the corner. My inclination was to run. Not wanting to be fired, I chose to stay. I lifted the guillotine door again, and to my relief Ivan was in view. He was a creature of routine, and he always spent the first hour of his morning pacing. His pattern was L-shaped. He would walk from the door five steps straight out and then turn right for three steps. He would then rock back and forth and come back to the guillotine door, which he would bump with his head. He would repeat that cycle for one hour and then rest.

I timed his pacing cycle and determined that I had seventeen seconds to run down the hallway and shut the open door. I staked my life on his consistency. He didn't seem to notice the wide-open door, which was unusual. Animals tend to notice any changes in their environment.

I decided that when he made his next turn, I would run down the L-shaped concrete hallway hoping upon hope that I would not see Ivan.

He turned and I ran. With every step my knees weakened. My heart pounded so hard I felt sure it would burst from fear. I made the corner and faced the critical moment. Ivan was still out of sight; I lunged for the door handle. As I reached out for the handle, I looked to the right. There was the bear, eight feet away. Our eyes met. His were cold and unfeeling and I'm sure mine expressed all the terror that filled the moment. I pulled the huge steel door with all my strength. It clanged shut and the clasp was secured. My knees buckled and I fell to the floor racked with the effects of too much adrenaline. I looked up and Ivan was staring at me through the viewing window of the hallway door.

I had almost let out a bear—the worst bear at the zoo.

Recently, our church family studied disciplines that could help us stand firm in our faith. The development of good habits is one of the keys to our becoming mature. Consider Hebrews 5:14:

> But solid food is for the mature, who because of practice have their senses trained to discern good and evil.

Consistent living produces its own protection. Seek it. Cherish it. Desire it. It may keep you from letting out a bear.

Back-Up Man

I always felt good about going into a cage with Bob Pedersen. He was the best back-up man in the business. I was sure that if something went wrong during a dangerous animal capture Bob would be there to do whatever was needed to bail me out. He felt comfortable with my abilities, and we really enjoyed working together.

When it is necessary to go into a cage and capture a potentially dangerous animal, the first rule of thumb is that there must always be two or more people to handle the animal effectively. The first man works the animal into position while the back-up man cuts off its avenues of escape. The roles can change back and forth when the animal changes position, but we usually decide who will catch and who will grab before we unlock the cage door.

Bob had excellent reaction time and he was strong. We netted and held everything from baboons to cheetahs, and

28

neither of us ever sustained an injury when working together. In fact, the only time that I sustained any injuries
was when I broke the cardinal rules of capture: 1) Never
go into a cage alone, and 2) Never work with an inexperi-
enced back-up.

It was a lazy summer afternoon in August and I had
finished all that I had been assigned around the health
center. I needed to get down to the North American section to vaccinate the arctic foxes for distemper, hepatitis,
and leptospirosis. They were overdue. I picked up the
phone to call the section, then set it down again as a young
and beautiful Ph.D. candidate from a local university
walked into the health center office. She glanced around,
then asked me if there was anybody who could help her. I
told her that I would if I could. She explained that she was
doing a behavioral study on white-handed gibbon apes and
needed to mark them with white paint so that she could
readily tell which ape was which.

We drove down to the Eurasian section and I looked
for the keeper who cared for the gibbons. He had already
gone home for the day and I couldn't find anyone else who
worked in the section. I noticed that the beautiful young
scientist kept checking her watch.

"Running late?" I queried.

"Yes, and I was so hoping that we would be able to get
the marking done today," she replied. She sounded so des-
perate, like maybe she wouldn't get her Ph.D. or maybe she
would get an "F" on her assignment or something like that.

"It's just that I can't find anybody to do back-up and
I'm not supposed to go into a capture situation alone," I
explained.

"Gee, I'm really sorry to be putting you to so much
trouble. Your gibbons must be more aggressive than the
ones at the primate center. Ours were easy. I even helped.
Hey, I would be glad to help you. I'll be your back-up."

"I'm sorry, I can't let you help. If you got bit, I'd get
fired," I explained.

She sat there looking so disappointed, so dejected. I had to prove that chivalry was not dead, so I made a stupid decision.

"I guess it wouldn't hurt anything to try," I announced.

"Oh, thank you, thank you, thank you. You're a dear."

Perhaps "dunce" would have been a more appropriate word, but just for a minute there I felt like a dear. And it felt pretty good. I gathered the capture equipment together and carried it to the back of the gibbon cage. All three of the gibbons looked at the two hoop nets I was carrying and hooted their displeasure. Hand-over-hand they quickly retreated to the far end of the cage and huddled together for mutual comfort. They looked fairly intimidated, and I took that to be a good sign.

I entered the cage with confidence. I had learned to act confident whether I felt confident or not. It gave you a slight edge if the animals were on the defensive. I left one of the two nets leaning against the cage wall and began to make my advance. The apes headed in different directions and it looked like it would be every gibbon for itself. I made a beautiful pass of the net, and whoosh! I had a gibbon. I knew that it must have looked impressive and I twisted the net to make sure that the gibbon didn't accomplish a premature exit.

It was about that time that the other two attacked me with a vengeance. I couldn't have engendered more wrath if I had tried. The two remaining gibbons seemed to be coming at me from every direction at the same time. One got a large handful of my hair and decided to keep it. The other gibbon grabbed my arm with such force that he caused an impressive bruise. I wore it for more than a week. There is no dignified way to exit a cage while being swarmed by gibbons. I just did the best I could to get out without being bitten to pieces. That was exactly what the Flying Gibbonski Brothers had in mind. As I fell backward into the holding cage, the beautiful young scientist had the presence of mind to push the sliding door shut. The gib-bons continued to reach through the chain link, hoping to pull me back out where they could work me over good. But I had backed just out of their reach.

Now there is really nothing clever that one can say when one has just proven himself to be a jerk, but one usually tries to say something. I know I did.

"Well, Miss, do you think this might be why they rec-ommend that we never go into a cage by ourselves?"

"Maybe so," she answered with a smile that convinced me that I had looked as ridiculous as I felt.

I would have been grateful if we just could have left and forgotten that the whole thing had happened, but there was still the little matter of the one gibbon that I had netted. It was still neatly twisted and bagged and lying qui-etly on the cool cement floor. "Be sure your sins will find you out," I thought. I had no choice. I had to get someone to help me release the gibbon and retrieve the nets. I managed to get my supervisor to come back with me, and together we quickly accomplished what I had failed to do alone.

"Next time you break the rules to impress somebody you may lose a finger, an eye, or your life. Don't do that anymore, Richmond," he said sternly. We drove back to the health center silently, and I pondered my irresponsible actions. I never made that same mistake again. But I did make others.

We had just hired Dr. Reed, a brand new veterinarian who had just graduated from vet school. Dr. Reed had never worked with wild animals, and capture was some-thing she had seen on television but had never participated in herself. She was nevertheless my supervisor, and I felt obligated to indulge her requests. She wanted to get some practice at capture, so she asked if I would please step aside to let her grab an adolescent greater kudu. A kudu is one of the largest antelopes, and though this young male only weighed a little over a hundred pounds he could still accomplish some serious damage with his formidable hooves. Dr. Reed would make the initial grab and control the head, the neck, and the front legs. She must keep it from falling to the ground or it would be in a great position to kick somebody's head off. I was back-up, and my job was to control the hindquarters and keep it on its hind feet. The hindquarters are the business end, the end that can deliver the most damage.

Dr. Reed rushed in and exhibited a good deal of pluck as she grabbed the young kudu. I grabbed the hindquarters and our veterinary intern began to inject a large dose of penicillin. It was then that Dr. Reed lost her grip, and in trying to regain it she actually tipped the animal upside down. The kudu kicked upward with all of its might and knocked me temporarily unconscious. The hoof had passed through my open mouth and connected with the rear teeth on the opposite side of my head. My gums were bleeding profusely and all I could hear was a loud ringing in my ear. When things began to make sense again Dr. Reed was saying, "Tell me where you are. Tell me your name." After I had convinced her that I had fully returned to coherency, I was removed for medical treatment.

I made a decision that I would never again work without an experienced back-up or lead. I stuck to that decision for the last two years of my zoo career, and to my memory, I was never injured in a capture situation again.

So much of life lived at its best is a matter of surrounding ourselves with people who will provide good back-up. They will pull us out of trouble when we get into a mess. They will remind us that we are out of line and need to be playing by the rules. They will pour courage into us so that we can perform to the limits of our potential.

Because we reap what we sow it is necessary that we learn to be good back-up ourselves. The following is a list of responsibilities that go with being a good back-up person. If you have learned to love yourself and put yourself first, then you need not apply for this position, because it requires willingness to sacrifice and courage enough to live for others. The Christian version of back-up is called "one anothering." As you read the following list, think of people in your life who are good at watching out for and caring for others.

John 15:12	Love one another.
Romans 5:13	Don't pass judgment on one another.
Romans 12:5	Be members of one another.
Romans 12:10	Be devoted to one another.
Romans 12:10	Honor one another.
Romans 12:16	Live in harmony with one another.
Romans 14:19	Build up one another.
Romans 15:5	Be like-minded toward one another.
Romans 15:7	Accept one another.
1 Corinthians 6:6	Don't make lawsuits against one another.
1 Corinthians 12:25	Care for one another.
Galatians 5:13	Serve one another in love.
Galatians 5:15	Don't spitefully hurt one another.
Galatians 5:26	Don't provoke or envy one another.
Galatians 6:2	Bear one another's burdens.
Ephesians 4:32	Be kind to one another.
Ephesians 4:32	Forgive one another.
Ephesians 5:21	Submit to one another.
Colossians 3:9	Don't lie to one another.
Colossians 3:13	Teach and counsel one another.
1 Thessalonians 3:12	Abound in love toward one another.
1 Thessalonians 4:18	Comfort one another.
Titus 3:3	Don't hate one another.
Hebrews 3:13	Encourage one another.
Hebrews 10:24	Stir up one another to love and good deeds.
James 4:11	Don't slander one another.
James 5:9	Don't bear grudges against one another.
James 5:16	Confess your sins to one another.
James 5:16	Pray for one another.

1 Peter 4:9	Offer hospitality to one another.
1 Peter 5:14	Greet one another.
1 John 1:7	Have fellowship with one another.

Now that you've read the responsibilities of the ideal back-up person, try to think of the people in your life who fill that responsibility for you. Why don't you write or call them and thank them? They deserve it.

As you read through the list, did you see any verse that best stated some area of strength that you possess and use to support others? Was there a weak area?

Close the book and thank God for the back-up people in your life and your area of strength, and ask Him to help you grow in some specific area where you now show a weakness.

Nowhere to Go

If you think a South American jaguar is impressive when she bares her teeth and snarls from the confines of her cage, you should see her just after she's escaped. It's an experience that will continue to haunt you for weeks to come.

I was sitting at my desk updating the lowland gorilla's polio immunization records one afternoon when one of the guards from the zoo security force called.

"We've got ourselves an emergency," blurted the head of the security force. "A big cat got out of her cage and attacked a keeper. We need you and your boss right now!"

I ran for the lab where Dr. Bernstein was checking test results with our lab technician.

"We've got a hot one, Doc. Big cat's loose in the South American section. Probably a jaguar. Keeper's been hurt."

He nodded and we grabbed our emergency gear and headed for the truck. You know that these things will happen occasionally but you never feel quite prepared when they do. We made speculation on who might have been hurt and hoped it was not too serious. A senior keeper ran to meet us as soon as the truck screeched to a halt in back of the jaguar exhibit. He filled us in while we got our equipment together. "Jaguar's loose, Doc. We'll need her tranquilized. She jumped Whittle. Looks like he'll be okay but his arm's broken. When the jag jumped him, he got his arm in her mouth. Security is taking him to the hospital now."

"Where's the public?" I inquired. It was 4:15 on a Monday afternoon. There wouldn't be a crowd, but there would be a few people wandering around.

"Yeah, we thought of that too. We rounded them up and locked them in the restrooms till we get the cat."

"Good idea."

"Let's go get her before she does any more damage," said the doctor.

The jaguar had been contained in a most original and primitive way. Several animal keepers had rushed to the scene and were directed to bring trash can lids and rakes. They surrounded the animal, then yelled and beat the trash can lids whenever she attempted to leave the area. It looked like a scene more suited to India at the turn of the century than Los Angeles in the early seventies.

We began to prepare the tranquilizer dart, carefully measuring the proper dose to bring the jaguar down. The dangers of shooting her with the dart were as follows: 1) Big cats don't fall asleep right away. With the proper dosage, the drop time would be about five minutes. 2) A high percentage of the darts misfire and don't inject anything but fatty tissue. You have to wait quite a while before you can shoot again because the animal may have received a full dose that is seeping out of a deep layer of fat. 3) Some animals get very angry when you shoot them with a dart because it is a very large gauge needle and it causes a fair amount of pain.

Now it stands to reason that all of these things are much more significant when the animal is outside the cage. She would be inclined to attack someone, most likely the one who had shot her with the rifle. That would be me. To be very honest, my mouth was dry, my heart was pounding, and I was shaking so hard that I wished someone would adjust my vertical hold. I raised the gun to my shoulder and began to zero in on the most muscular area of her hindquarters. She looked at me and I stopped breathing for a second. I would pull the trigger when she looked away.

The silence was shattered by the arrival of our assistant director, Dr. Nathan Gale.

"Don't shoot!" he yelled with firm authority.

I lowered the gun and he joined us for a brief conference.

"Listen guys, she just wants back in her cage. If we shoot her and the dart misfires she might run for the hills. If she gets loose in Griffith Park it might take a week to find her. The police would want her shot and we don't want that. Let's just apply gentle pressure and guide her back to her cage. When she sees the open door she'll run in."

I repeated an axiom to myself, "The boss may not always be right, but the boss is always the boss." Then I said, "Gee, it's worth a try. We haven't got anything to lose." I hoped I sounded less skeptical than I felt.

Dr. Gale had a couple of keepers run ahead and open the door to her cage. He organized the rest of us into two lines so that we formed a corridor through which she would walk. Then he took the dangerous position. He began to slowly put pressure on her by moving closer and closer. She snarled and swiped but he stood his ground. Finally she began to move. He applied constant and even pressure, not enough to challenge her but not so little that she would stop. It went so smoothly that it began looking like a man out for a walk with his pet jaguar. But the most difficult moment was still ahead. Would she go easily through the door to her cage? Not only did she go easily; she actually became excited and ran to get back in her cage. This defied reason and logic. Something inside of me had told me that she wanted her freedom, and that hadn't turned out to be the case at all.

I couldn't help but admire Dr. Gale's courage, but I was more intrigued with how he seemed to know how the jaguar would respond when she saw her cage. So I asked Dr. Gale, "How did you know what she would do?"

His answer was great. "Well, you never really know for sure what a wild animal will do and that's why we call them wild. But you can make a good guess based on Heine Hediger's book, *Psychology and Behavior of Animals in Zoos and Circuses*. Hediger's thesis is that an animal's perspective changes as soon as he leaves his territory or home—his cage, if you will. He quickly senses that he has nowhere to run. He has no sense of his surroundings; to him it's unfamiliar territory. He becomes insecure. Home represents security, so it becomes the desired destination."

"Would this method always be the best choice?" I questioned.

"I stay away from 'always' answers, but I do believe it would usually be the best method to try first."

We humans are not so different from the jaguar. I remembered back to my own childhood when I had decided to run away. My mother had spanked me for some justifiable reason and I became indignant. I announced that I was going to run away and she offered to help me pack. She even made an excellent lunch for me. I stood by as she neatly folded my clothes and laid them in the suitcase. She snapped it closed and handed it to me along with the lunch bag. We walked together, she and I, to the end of our driveway. I looked first to the right and then to the left. The world seemed larger and more threatening than I had remembered it and my eyes filled with tears. I began to sob and my mother asked kindly what was making me cry.

"I don't know where to go!" I wailed.

"Would you like to go home?" she said.

"Yes."

"You know that means you'll have to be good, don't you?"

"Yes." (My mother would believe anything.)

She let me come home, and feelings of relief and security welled up from deep within my five-year-old soul.

Have you read the story of the Prodigal Son recently? It may be found in the fifteenth chapter of the Gospel of Luke. The son becomes increasingly unhappy in the faraway country and he begins to long for home. Home represents the presence of his father, and he senses that the proper attitude is humility and subjection. The father's response is affection and complete acceptance. We must never forget that the father always loved the son, even when the son was in the faraway country. Let us also never forget that the son was not allowed to perform any nonsense at all underneath the roof of the father. Peace and security are reserved for those who keep their mind on the Lord.

> Open the gates,
> that the righteous nation which keeps faith
> may enter in.
> Thou dost keep him in perfect peace,
> whose mind is stayed on thee,
> because he trusts in thee.
> Trust in the LORD for ever,
> for the LORD GOD
> is an everlasting rock.
>
> Isaiah 26:2–4

My friend, if you're home, stay home. If you're not, come home. There was an occasion when Jesus offended many who had been following Him. The Bible tells us that many withdrew and stopped walking with Him. "Jesus said to the twelve, 'Do you also wish to go away?' Simon Peter answered him, 'Lord, to whom shall we go? You have the words of eternal life'" (John 6:67–68).

In the words of J. B. Coats's hymn, "Where could I go but to the Lord?"

Easy to Grab,

Hard to Let Go

Don't you just hate king cobras? I know I do—and I came by my feeling honestly. Our zoo had a thirteen-foot giant that seemed to me to be the embodiment of evil. He had a scar over his left eye that made him look mean and, more significantly, kept him from shedding his skin in a normal fashion. At least twice a year we would get the dreaded phone call from the reptile house: "The cobra shed his skin last week, but the eye cap didn't come off. Looks infected. Suppose you and the doc could come down and clean it?"

A snake's skin includes a clear scale over the eye to protect it from sand and foreign objects. Snakes have no eyelids, so they have no way to blink for protection. The snake's scar prevented a normal shed, so the eye cap needed to be surgically removed.

We made the appointment for the next day. Arrangements were more critical for this procedure because of its extreme danger. Only two people at the zoo could take responsibility for grabbing the more deadly snakes, and this was the most deadly. This snake's venom glands contain enough poison to kill one thousand adults—a fact that seemed to come up every time we did this procedure.

The curator of reptiles was assigned to grab the head, and two reptile keepers were to steady the body. When the snake was subdued, the veterinarian would begin the delicate surgery. His arena kept him inches from a lethal injection. My job was to furnish scalpel, sponge, hemostat, and anything else to expedite the procedure.

The capture of the cobra was as follows: The five of us took our positions. The two keepers stood on either side of the large cage door. The curator stood in front of the door about six feet away. The vet and I stood on either side of the curator about ten feet from the door. The keepers' only defense were sheer bird nets with two-foot handles.

With a nod of his head, the curator signaled for the door to be opened. Seconds later the king cobra appeared. As soon as he saw us, he stopped, spread his cape, and raised to full stature. The cage was two feet off the ground, so we were all looking at the snake at eye level. The cobra was trembling with excitement as he, in turn, stared at each of his five enemies. He seemed to be choosing who would be his prey. The curator was chosen, and with shocking quickness the snake lunged forward, hissing and growling with malevolent rage. With lightning speed, the skilled keepers placed the sheer nets over the snake's head. And as he pushed to get through, the curator firmly grasped his neck just behind his venom sacs. The keepers grabbed the writhing body, then the curator nodded and said, "Let's get this over with."

The pressure was incredible. The vet's hands were trembling and beads of sweat began to run down the curator's forehead. The curator turned to me and said, "Do you have any cuts or scratches on your hands?"

I looked and said, "No."

"Get a wad of paper towels, quick," he followed in a strained voice. I did so.

"Now, put it in the cobra's mouth."

The king watched the paper towels as they were carefully positioned to allow him to bite them. He bit down violently and began to chew. The towels became yellow with venom until they began to drip.

The curator continued, "Did you know several elephants die every year from king cobra bites? A man could never survive a bite with a full load of venom. That's why I'm having you drain his venom sacs. My hands are sweaty and my fingers are cramping. When I let him go, it may not be quick enough. More people are bitten trying to let go of snakes than when they grab them. You get weak quickly when you grab a big poisonous snake."

There are many situations in life that are parallels—easy to grab, hard to let go—so it pays to think twice before you grab them. Indebtedness, vengeance, lying, adultery, drugs, alcohol, pornography, promiscuity—these and many more are serpents that will drain your strength and bite you to death while you're trying to let them go.

> There is a way which seems right to a man, but its end is the way of death.
>
> Proverbs 14:12

Samson found that embracing Delilah was easy and exciting. But his life was destroyed after he laid his head on her lap. Reread his story in chapters 13–16 of the Book of Judges. Ask yourself two questions:

1. "Who do I know who has his head on Delilah's lap?" If you know someone who does, attempt a rescue.

2. "If I woke up on Delilah's lap, would there be anyone to rescue me?" If not, make the type of friends who would try.

Free As a Bird

It didn't make sense to me. The criminals were as free as a bird and the birds were in jail. It probably doesn't make sense to you either. Let me explain.

When I was first transferred to the zoo health center, I found myself caring for a cage full of red-tailed hawks. There were fifteen of them, and they were crowded together in a pitifully small cage. To my eye, they looked to be very depressed. I inquired as to the reason why we might be caring for fifteen red-tailed hawks off exhibit and the answer really frosted me.

The senior keeper, an extremely jovial Mexican-American man by the name of Johnny Torres, said, "Eeeeeeh, those hawks are evidence for court trials. These guys caught them illegally and we keep them here until their trial is over."

47

"What happens when the court trials are over?" I asked.

"I don't know," he answered. "We never hear. Some of these birds have been here a long time. We don't even know which bird goes with what trial. So they'll probably die here."

"That doesn't make sense to me," I protested.

"Richmond, did somebody lie to you and tell you things make sense around here? It's best not to ask too many questions about this either. The guys down below, down in administration, they don't like to know that they got problems. So my advice is to drop it."

Well, to tell you the truth, it just wasn't in my nature to drop it. After all, it was the sixties and this was a cause. It seemed to me that the poor, the children, and the animals needed help, and this was injustice pure and simple. The poachers were free and the poachees were being punished.

I inquired gently and became convinced that the birds were in trouble. Nobody cared about their plight, and the red tape to get them released was so sticky that no one would wade through it.

There was really only one answer. They must be let go. But it must look like an accident. The punishment for letting low-risk animals out was nothing more than a notice to correct a deficiency. I had never received one before, but it would be a small price to pay to right this wrong.

I decided that I would let them go on a Tuesday afternoon when the supervisors were at the animal health committee meeting. They would be out of the area for about two hours, more than enough time to accomplish my mission.

Tuesday came and the supervisors left the hospital area. I made my way out to the cage, slipped the lock out of the hasp, and left the door wide open. I looked around. There was no one in sight. I slipped back into the health center and set about my duties with a profound sense of fulfillment, an abiding feeling of satisfaction. It was not to last.

After one hour I decided to check the cage. Astonishment, disbelief, wonder, and confusion reigned supreme as I beheld all fifteen birds still in the cage relaxing. There was still time. Perhaps the red-tails just needed some inspiration. Well, I knew what would be inspirational. I ran into their cage waving my arms and growled like a bear. That inspired them, all right. They flew out of the cage and landed not ten feet from the cage door. The look that they gave me was pitiful. They were confused and it was clear to me that they wanted back into the cage. "Don't you see the sky?" I pleaded. "That's what you were meant for." I began feeling a little self-conscious inside the cage so I stepped out to finish my address. "What's wrong with you? You're not chickens. You're majestic birds of prey. You hunt your food. God gave you a purpose, now go fulfill it." I decided to go back to the health center. Maybe their instincts would take over and they would feel some primal urge to command the wind. I left for fifteen minutes and then returned. Not one bird had felt any urges. In fact, some had walked back into the cage. With fifteen minutes to go, I gave up. I don't mind telling you I was more than a little deflated. I ended up herding the birds back into the cage like goats. Where had I gone wrong?

I had approached their problem anthropomorphically, which is a fancy way of saying I was projecting my thoughts into the minds of the birds. The birds had not been sitting in the cage longing to be free. Those were my thoughts. They had long since become satisfied with just waiting to be fed. No famines to suffer. No droughts to survive. No territorial battles to enjoin. It wasn't all bad. *I* felt bad, but *they* didn't. The reason I felt bad was because by caging them we had taken something from them that they needed to be noble—their purpose. God had created the red-tailed hawks to hunt rodents and reptiles. Few birds can equal their elegant flight or fearless pursuit of prey. This group of birds had been robbed of their ecological purpose. And we weren't even letting the zoo patrons appreciate them. That's what was bothering me.

I thought a bit more about freedom as I finished my responsibilities that day. I concluded that freedom was the ability to fulfill the purpose for which you were created. I further reasoned that man had an interesting distinction. Unlike the animals, man can never be kept from fulfilling his purpose. He is always and in every circumstance free to perform the function for which he was created. Man's purpose is to love and to serve God. The more difficult the circumstances, the greater the opportunity to achieve that purpose. We are now and will always be free to be what we were meant to be, that creature designed to glorify God and enjoy Him forever.

Solomon, the wisest man that ever lived, put it this way:

> The end of the matter; all has been heard. Fear God, and keep his commandments; for this is the whole duty of man. For God will bring every deed into judgment, with every secret thing, whether good or evil.
>
> Ecclesiastes 12:13–14

The apostle Paul shares in Galatians 5:1:

> For freedom Christ has set us free . . . .

In verse 13 he further states:

> For you were called to freedom, brethren; only do not use your freedom as an opportunity for the flesh, but through love be servants of one another.

Are you fulfilling the purpose for which you were created? Or have you become satisfied with the ways of the world? You have the freedom to choose.

You'd Better Sit Down

I was preparing a surgical pack in the zoo's well-stocked operating room when I was called to the phone. "Richmond, I hear the vets are at a conference and won't be back until this afternoon." I recognized the voice of the senior keeper at the children's zoo.

"That's right, Bill. Is something up?"

"Yeah! We have these raccoon kittens down here and they are both showing signs of losing the use of their hind legs. It's the darndest thing. We've never seen anything like this."

"Would you like me to pick them up? I could keep them up here until the vets get back from the conference. They will probably need to do some testing and take X-rays anyway."

"That would be great, Richmond. Then if they have

something hot they won't be passing it around down here. Let's go for it."

I drove right down and picked them up. It was about 9:30 in the morning. I took them out of their carrying cage when I got back to the health center and confirmed that they were indeed losing the use of their hind legs.

Raccoon kittens are extremely appealing. These had been hand raised and were both very playful and affectionate. They seemed all right except for the extreme weakness in their hind legs, so I placed them in the two large pockets of my lab coat. As I puttered from room to room I played with the little bandits. They loved to chew on my fingers and wrestle with my hands. But they soon tired and napped a good deal more than normal. When they woke they refused to eat and played a bit less enthusiastically than they had in the morning. I felt sorry for them so I stayed in contact with them the whole day long.

It was about four o'clock when the veterinarians returned. Dr. Bill Hulsizer came in first. He found me in the X-ray room, and the color drained from his face when he saw the raccoon kittens in my pockets.

"Are they losing the use of their legs?" he asked in a most serious tone.

"How'd you know? You haven't even looked at them," I declared in genuine astonishment.

He lifted the young raccoons out of my pockets and placed them in a stainless steel cage onto a bath towel. "You'd better sit down, Gary. You're not going to be too happy about what I'm about to tell you."

I sat down wondering what I had done wrong. I couldn't think of anything, but that didn't stop me from wondering.

He looked me right in the eye and said, "I'm about 90 percent sure both the kittens have rabies."

"What?" I exclaimed in disbelief. "How could you know? You haven't even examined them."

Bill began to tell me a story that surprised and hurt

me very much. He shared that our other veterinarian, Dr. Westfall, had given the raccoon kittens a modified live rabies vaccine as what she thought should be a standard procedure to protect them. She did not realize that, even though it prevents rabies in dogs, such a vaccine can *cause* rabies in raccoons. Bill said that he had discovered this serious error while he was reviewing the medical records at the children's zoo. He had confronted Dr. Westfall immediately, and she was very embarrassed about her lack of knowledge. She insisted that she would handle the situation her own way and asked Bill to back off as if he didn't know a thing. Unfortunately, that's exactly what he did. She discovered a statistic that indicated that there was a chance the raccoons would not come down with rabies at all, so she decided to play the odds. She even went as far as erasing the medical records at the children's zoo. Both vets checked the raccoons two to three times a day, but they never mentioned anything to me. They didn't count on the raccoons coming down with rabies the one day that they were both away at a conference.

"How can you be sure they have the disease?" I challenged. "They're not foaming at the mouth."

"They have the more common symptoms. What we call the mute form of the disease."

"Does this mean that I will have to go through the series of shots that I've always heard about?" I asked.

"That depends on whether or not you have experienced vital contact. If you have been bitten or your skin has been broken or scratched, that is vital contact. If you had any open sores that their saliva might have entered, that would be vital contact. In the case of the baby raccoons, it would be considered vital if they so much as scratched you because these little guys put their paws in their mouths so much. Let's see your hands."

My hands were covered with nicks and scratches, about half of which they had caused that day. Bill nodded and said, "I think you'll want to take the treatment."

I felt sick. I would now be finding out if the treatment was worthy of its horrible reputation.

The raccoon kittens were sacrificed and their brains were sent to two different labs for analysis. Both labs confirmed rabies. A thorough investigation was launched to determine who might have sustained vital contact with the raccoons. One hundred and twenty people had been exposed, but only five in a vital way. There were two children's zoo attendants, the zoo's photographer and his assistant, and me. One of the children's zoo attendants refused to take the treatment for personal reasons, so as it turned out only four of us met to take the hard road together.

Forty hours after exposure we were driven to County General Hospital. The first matter of business was to determine if we were strong enough to endure the treatment. They gave each of us a thorough physical, and we all proved to be of sound body. Then they told us that 3 percent of the people who took the treatment died from it. Of course each of us thought we might be in that 3 percent, and one of us was nearly correct.

We were given other statistics that spelled out our chances. If we were punctured by a rabid animal there was a fifty-fifty chance that we would come down with the disease. If we came down with the disease, there was a 100 percent chance that we would die from it. We were also warned that one out of the four of us might experience a violent allergic reaction to the massive dose of horse serum we were about to receive.

Then the treatment began. They decided that my dose of horse serum would be fifty cc.'s. The syringe and needle looked like an outlandish prop from a bizarre comedy, but let me assure you that it was not funny. I hope I shall never receive that large a dose of anything ever again. It hurt tremendously, and sitting down was out of the question for hours to come.

They led us into another room and we began the series

to the abdominal area. They chose that area because we use the least amount of muscles there. Rabies shots, in addition to being painful, are also somewhat complicated. First, a map is drawn to direct where the doctor will administer the shots. He writes the numbers one through twenty-three right on the abdomen in indelible ink. That way he will not give the shots in the same place twice. The shots are carefully administered subcutaneously (between the muscles and the skin). Then the swelling begins and the severe soreness sets in.

Shots one and two were given. They were very painful. The burning pain lasted about two minutes and gave way to soreness and intense itching. But it was bearable, and we began to encourage each other during each administration.

We met at the zoo every morning and were driven to the hospital. The hospital is not an architectural triumph, and it resides in a depressed area of Los Angeles. It seemed grey, gloomy, and institutional, especially stark after leaving the gardenlike atmosphere of the zoo in Griffith Park.

The four of us became good friends and determined that we ought to make the best of a bad thing. We would all take turns pretending to foam at the mouth and trying to bite one of the others. I shared that this experience would be great to tell our grandchildren in years to come—it may even make a good story for a book someday. When I discovered that my blood was going to be valuable and could be sold after I completed the treatment, I was overjoyed. I shared my discovery with the others the next morning. Karen, the children's zoo attendant that was with us, said, "Gary you're making this sound like we have just had one big stroke of luck. It's not that good," she added.

Karen was not at the zoo to meet us for our fifth day of treatment. She had been admitted to the hospital the night before. So after we received our ninth and tenth shots, we went up to her room to see her. She was covered with a fiery red rash and her face was very puffy. We managed to cheer her up some, but all of us were finding it hard to be good little soldiers. The course of treatment was making us all tired. I had a constant headache and was nauseous most of the time. We were all experiencing a good deal of swelling and itched fiercely all of the time. The doctors said that these symptoms were good signs. It meant that our bodies were fighting the virus. I knew my body was fighting back, but I wished it was not the battleground as well.

I was not up to working on the sixth day and my wife, Carol, insisted on driving me straight to the hospital. On the way my fingers began to swell and hives began to appear everywhere. The doctors were a bit concerned, but they felt that the symptoms could be controlled with medication. So they let me go home.

A few hours later Carol drove me back to County General, and they admitted me quickly. The medication hadn't helped at all.

I was becoming very ill with a ravaging case of serum sickness. The swelling progressed until I was unrecognizable. I couldn't bend my fingers and it was painful to touch anything. The itching was fiery and incredible. No pain that I have ever encountered before or since compares to the sensations that I felt during that twenty-four hours of hell. I felt trapped in the dimensions of my own body. There is not a torture chamber on earth that could have punished me more severely. It was difficult to breathe, and I was racked with nausea and retching constantly. I stayed coherent during the whole ordeal and saw the concerned look on the doctors' faces in the intensive care unit. I knew that I was in trouble and prayed constantly for relief. I repeated the name of Jesus over and over and I felt His presence with me.

I thought that I might be dying and I was afraid. I wasn't so afraid for myself, but I didn't want to leave Carol alone with our two little girls, Marci and Wendi. I begged the Lord to make the feelings go away, but they didn't. I watched the hospital clock from my position on the gurney. Minutes seemed like hours, and hours seemed like years. It got to a point where the pain was so intense that I lost my resolve to live. I prayed, "Take me, Lord, and I'll trust You to take care of my family." I really wanted to die, but still the night went on. I tried to think of the great saints and remembered Job. His trials lasted nearly a year, and he had continued to hang in there. I remembered Jeremiah who had come to the end and proclaimed that the Lord was his sufficiency. Then I remembered the apostle Paul and what he had written to the church at Philippi:

> . . . that I may know Him and the power of His resurrection, and may share His sufferings, becoming like Him in His death . . . .
>
> Philippians 3:10

A tremendous peace settled in as I realized I had been given a chance to know Christ in a different way than I had ever known Him before. He had suffered because of my sin, and now I was suffering because of someone else's sin. We had something in common now, and it helped me to know something about His powers of love that added to His greatness. He chose to suffer for me before I had loved Him in any way. There were only a handful of people I would be willing to suffer for, and all of them already loved me. How different Jesus was from me. How better. How perfect.

I resigned to the will of Jesus and He waited there with me.

I asked to talk to my wife in case it would be the last time I would get the chance. I was getting weaker by the minute. I told her that I wanted her to know that I loved her. She knew something was probably really wrong because I tend not to say that nearly as much as I should.

By morning there was a blessed relief that let me know that I was going to live. I thanked the Lord.

Dr. Westfall never apologized for her actions which almost cost us our lives, but I still forgave her gladly and freely because of what Jesus taught me during our night of horrors together.

> Therefore since we are justified by faith, we have peace with God through our Lord Jesus Christ. Through him we have obtained access to this grace in which we stand, and we rejoice in our hope of sharing the glory of God. More than that we rejoice in our sufferings, knowing that our sufferings produce endurance, and endurance produces character, and character produces hope, and hope does not disappoint us, because God's love has been poured into our hearts by the Holy Spirit which has been given to us.
>
> Romans 5:1–5

Now that's Good News.

The Best Chimp I Have Ever Known

I will never forget Charlie. As chimps go, he was the best. Charlie was the dominant chimp of our collection and well loved by any whose privilege it had been to care for him. Charlie was a peacemaker.

The Los Angeles Zoo had eight chimps that formed a cohesive group. They were tight because they had a leader that didn't put up with any monkey business. Charlie spent a good deal of time keeping his group at peace, and that was no easy assignment. Toto and Jeanie were a part of his group. Toto was a former circus chimp and stirred up trouble whenever he could. He would often hoot and scream and charge his cage mates. He would then slap them with the back of his hand and run away. Then Toto would make dramatic and threatening gestures, and that's when Charlie would swing into action.

He was a little lighter than Toto but had long since

established who was boss. Charlie would charge Toto and hold him down and scream at him. Toto would act submissive and Charlie would let him off the hook. In no time, Toto would be back to his old tricks, but Charlie never gave up on Toto. He tried his best, but Toto was a hopeless case.

Jeanie was no gift, either. She was always on the edge of a fit and very unpredictable. But Charlie was equal to all of his responsibilities. He was truly an exceptional chimpanzee.

One day a decision was made to remodel the very inadequate chimpanzee exhibit. It was also decided that the eight chimps would be kept at the health center until the remodeling was completed. We divided the group in half and placed them in adjacent cages. I can't remember whether there was much thought as to how we should divide them, but rational or not, our plan turned out to be a disaster.

Toto and Jeanie were housed with two of the young chimps in one cage while Charlie was housed with the coquettish Annie, the beautiful Bonnie, and the always affectionate Judy. It should have been heaven for Charlie to be separated from Toto, but that's not how it turned out.

The months began to pass, and Toto quickly realized that Charlie could do little more than yell at him from the next cage. Charlie would try his best to govern his group from the next cage, but it was futile. Charlie started to lose a little weight and began to show signs of depression. One morning, we found that our beloved group leader had died during the night. He died sitting up, leaning against the side of the cage nearest to Toto's group.

I cannot describe to you the sadness that descended over the health center. We felt as if we had lost a good friend. We had. He was the best chimp I have ever known.

When we performed a clinical examination, we were crushed by what we discovered. Charlie had died of a perforated ulcer. Things had been bothering him a lot more than he had been letting on. Not being able to keep his family at peace had taken a terrible toll on him.

One of the problems that a veterinarian encounters is the inability of his patients to tell him where it hurts so that they can be helped. If only Charlie could have let us know, we would have done anything to help him.

One of the advantages we have over the animal kingdom is that we can let somebody know we need help. We can point to where it hurts. We can ask for help.

God's Word speaks to us directly about asking for what we need.

. . . your Father knows what you need before you ask him.

Matthew 6:8

Ask, and it will be given you; seek, and you will find; knock, and it will be opened to you. For every one who asks receives, and he who seeks finds, and to him who knocks it will be opened. Or what man of you, if his son asks him for bread, will give him a stone? Or if he asks for a fish, will give him a serpent? If you then, who are evil, know how to give good gifts to your children, how much more will your Father who is in heaven give good things to those who ask him!

Matthew 7:7–11

And whatever you ask in prayer, you will receive, if you have faith.

Matthew 21:22

Have you asked the Lord for anything lately? You may ask for help if you are in trouble. You may ask for forgiveness if you have sinned. You may ask for gifts, like love for others, patience, or wisdom. You may even ask for God to help a close friend. He commands us to ask. It is His nature to want to help us. That is what being a Father is all about.

The Mayor
Is Coming!

I came to dread the words "the mayor is coming." It wasn't that we were going to meet him. That would have been fun. Instead, it meant that we had to clean up the zoo in places where we didn't know we had places. We had to transform the zoo into an immaculate display for the mayor to see.

I remember once being made to clean up some building material behind an obscure barn in an obscure corner of the zoo. I offered my opinion that I didn't think the mayor would be coming behind this barn. The restroom facilities in the main zoo were perfectly acceptable.

My supervisor smiled. "Richmond," he said, "I'm paid to think. You are paid to do."

He must have been telling the truth, I thought, because I had never seen him do anything. I told him I didn't know what kind of money he made, but it must be a thrill to be so overpaid for his responsibility.

He smiled again and pointed to the back of the barn and motioned for me to go there. So we shoveled and hosed and scrubbed and scoured until each section virtually gleamed with purity. And then we waited. And waited. And waited. Finally, the zoo closed for the day and we all went home exhausted and a little irritated.

But that is how it was. I can recall at least ten occasions when the mayor was announced and he never came. He did come to the front of the zoo one day, however, to have his picture taken with fifteen children from the Taiwanese community who were bused in for a public relations shot. He gave a little speech about how he had been personally responsible for this marvelous zoo and then he kissed a child, sustaining the kiss until all flashbulbs had burnt themselves to smithereens. Then he walked away, completely unaware of the enormous manpower exerted on his behalf.

I inquired as to the possible reasons why he never actually came into the zoo, and was informed that he once had. Amazed, I asked what miracle had attracted him. Mark, one of our zoo's leading humorists, offered, "He must have caught the scent of cameras."

"It's the truth," offered another keeper. "He came to see the white rhinos, Sonny and Cher, let out for the first time. He made everybody wait until he arrived. When he got there he spent ten minutes looking for a place to stand where the television cameras would be sure to capture him when the rhinos made their first entrance. The mayor and his entourage climbed through wild roses and ankle deep ivy to stand on the hill just behind the exhibit. It turned out to be, as expected, the very best view for television. The mayor signaled the keeper to let the white rhinos out and filming began. Sonny snorted and pranced out in a thunderous manner, followed by his saucy mate. The crowd cheered and, as if trained, the rhinos stopped to consider their public right below the mayor. He couldn't have planned it better. But he did leave one important consideration to chance."

"What was that?" I asked in rapt attention.

"The automatic sprinklers," said the keeper, beginning to laugh hysterically. "They came on with a vengeance. The television news teams got it all. There were dignitaries running in every direction. They were soaked. It was great!"

"What did the mayor do?" I asked.

"He just left. I heard he was really bent out of shape. Anyway, I think that's why he doesn't come into the zoo anymore. He's probably still mad."

That story sort of made up for all the extra work we had to do, I thought.

In fairness, it occurred to me that perhaps we dreaded the mayor's "visits" because of the extra work. We might even have looked forward to his coming if we hadn't let things get so far behind. We shouldn't have let junk accumulate; there was no reason for it.

There is a King who will be coming and we have all been given notice. I'm sure you know that I am referring to the return of the Lord Jesus Christ. Many people have foolishly predicted the date, even though the Bible says that no man knows the time of His appearing. He will come unexpectedly, "like a thief in the night." And He will inspect us with an absolutely thorough review. Over and over the Bible cautions us to be ready, to prepare for His coming.

. . . there is laid up for me the crown of righteousness, which the Lord, the righteous judge, will award to me on that Day, and not only to me but also to all who have loved his appearing.

2 Timothy 4:8

The Mayor Is Coming!

The term "loved his appearing" has always intrigued me. That would be those who are ready and current in their walk with Jesus. The folks who have let a lot of waste material accumulate in their lives would dread the thought of His coming. How about you? Are you up to date? Or do you have some serious cleaning to do in your life?

I Never Realized

The arrival of a new rhinoceros at the Los Angeles Zoo turned out to be one of the most meaningful spiritual events in my life. Let me tell you about it.

One of the goals of a modern zoo is reproduction, especially of rare animals. This goal could not be realized with our black rhino collection because we owned only one male, Arthur. Arthur (King Arthur) was a young, robust, jaunty, temperamental male. But he needed a lady. We came through in a big way by our purchase of Lady Twinkle Toes, a dark, elusive beauty who pulsated with rhino charm.

She arrived at the zoo in a crate so large it could not be driven to the back of the exhibit because of the high bridges and tunnels that were a part of the back-road system. So the decision was made to lift the crate into the front of the exhibit with a large crane that stood waiting for her arrival. When she did arrive, it was clear she was very upset. On the same day, she had been taken from the cargo hold of a ship in her crate, lifted onto a truck, and driven forty miles over the Los Angeles freeway system to the zoo. The variety of smells, sounds, and shadows had taken their toll on an animal that is extremely subject to fear and anxiety. She was feeling progressively more trapped by the crate and she wanted out. NOW!

We knew this because she was frequently ramming the door of her massive crate so hard that we heard cracking and noticed splintering around the hinges. The order was shouted to hurry it up with the steel cables. There was a frenzy of activity as the cables were bolted together and attached to the giant hook at the end of the crane's cable. "Lift away!" The crate began to rise amidst hoorahs and the diesel roar that thundered from the crane. Billows of smoke belched forth from an engine that obviously needed more maintenance. Inside the crate Lady Twinkle Toes had long since reached her stress limit. She was possessed by terror, and in her mind her life was on the line. Her very survival was in question. Seventeen feet in the air, the crate began to rock violently. Four-by-fours bowed, cracked, and fell to the ground as the door began to disintegrate before our eyes. The crane operator swung the crate into position as quickly as possible while the rhino, with incredible strength, blasted the last vestiges of the door off its hinges.

We were terrified. If she attempted to jump from that height, she would be crushed and killed by her own weight. Rhinos see very poorly, and she stared downward without the focus or intelligence to interpret her circumstances. She was trembling with fright and her eyes were filled with tears. Ten feet, eight feet, six feet, four feet. Still four feet above the ground, Lady Twinkle Toes opted for freedom. She fell with a sickening thud and we waited, with bated breath and clenched teeth, hoping she would be able to get up. She snorted and struggled successfully to a standing position. Her body was trembling violently with colossal fear, the kind that produces rage. She noticed a large boulder that through tear-filled eyes looked like a man or another animal. She charged it mightily. When she hit it, it moved only slightly and she fell to her knees. Staggering again to her feet, she noticed another boulder and charged it. Again the impact brought her to her knees. This time she got up a little more slowly. Then the most amazing thing happened . . . her whole body began to glisten red in the morning sun. She seemed to be perspiring great drops of blood from every pore in her body.

I turned to the veterinarian and exclaimed, "Doctor, what's going on? I have never seen anything like this before!"

"This animal has reached a maximum of stress," he said. "Rhinos, hippos, and elephants under this kind of stress can burst capillaries all over their bodies. She can't take much more stress. She's in great danger."

We were all glad when she stopped her awesome displays of fear and rage and began to calm down. As I considered this marvel, the words of another doctor, the beloved physician Luke, echoed in my mind.

And being in agony he (Jesus) prayed more earnestly; and his sweat became like great drops of blood falling down upon the ground.

Luke 22:44

I thought, "Lord, I never realized. I never dreamed that You knew about stress in this way. How trapped You must have felt. How alone. You really can understand how I feel."

The Lord left us with two truths in this incident. It is good to reach out to friends during times of great stress;

but when they don't come through, God is always suffi-
cient. He will get us through. Jesus is into stress management. We read in Matthew 11:28–30:

> Come to me, all who labor and are heavy laden, and I
> will give you rest. Take my yoke upon you, and learn from
> me; for I am gentle and lowly in heart, and you will find rest
> for your souls. For my yoke is easy, and my burden is light.

Are you stressed? Take it to the Counselor first. Jesus un-
derstands.

Good for Something

There is a dark side to my nature that I must confess. Let me do that for the sake of a clear conscience. You see, I take an abnormal pleasure from incidents involving pompous people being made to look ridiculous. This is hard to admit, but is very true and probably not very pastoral ("Vengeance is Mine," saith the Lord). Let me share a story that perhaps best illustrates the pinnacle of joy I am capable of attaining.

In the early 1970s, the Los Angeles Zoo hired a brand new curator of mammals. She had no previous zoo experience and had never worked with mammals. However, she did have a Ph.D., and someone in a high place felt that was more than enough. Her doctorate was related to reptiles and amphibians, and her thesis was a study of how the environment of Central America affected the evolution of frogs. She was clearly coming from a highly academic approach to life which left her, for the most part, on the outside looking in regarding the animal-keeping staff.

My first contact with her was very revealing. She stormed into the health center and said, "I want you to open that door and hold down that chimp. I need to see his ear tattoo." She pointed at Toto. Now Toto was a former circus chimp who had become psychotic. At a hundred and fifty pounds, he was six times as strong as a man and would never submit to this kind of restraint. I gave her the benefit of the doubt and said, "You are kidding, aren't you?"

She bristled, "I am not!"

"Doctor, no combination of ten men could hold down that chimp. But if you find ten willing men, I'll open the door for them."

She stormed out.

She formed a good friendship with my supervisor, the zoo veterinarian, and came to the health center often. She made it clear to him that the only location in the zoo she found intellectually stimulating was in his presence. I'm not sure how she pulled it off, but I always felt like a Quasimodo or an Igor when she came for her visits. The veterinarian would also change his attitude toward me. I felt like the lowly help, not his right-arm assistant, while she was there. So I made it a point to get lost whenever she showed up.

Her first major assignment was to send a medium-size black bear to the Paris Zoo. She designed a shipping crate and sent the specifications to the maintenance crew for construction. On one of my journeys to Maintenance, I saw the nearly finished crate and inquired what it was for. I was told it was for the bear to go to Paris. It was one-inch plywood interlined with thin aluminum. I told the gentleman the bear would never leave the Los Angeles airport. He said he just built it to the specs; the curator had designed it. I saw her later that day and, in an effort to be helpful, said, "Doctor, the crate you had built will never leave LAX . . . the bear will tear it to pieces."

She looked at me as if I were a child and said, "I got my design from a book by the world authority on bears, and I'm quite confident this will do very nicely, thank you."

"I assure you, Doctor, the bear has never read the authority; and even if he had, he'd eat the crate anyway."

She stormed off.

When the day came, we tranquilized the bear and put him in the crate. We watched as the bear-laden truck headed for the airport. I left all the tranquilizing equipment in the truck on the strong hunch that I was right. The truck left at 10 A.M. and returned without the bear at noon. The keeper stayed long enough to know that the bear was waking up from the tranquilizer. If we were called, it would be before 1 P.M., which was air-freight departure. I was wrong; it was 1:05 P.M. A frantic voice, angry and afraid, demanded that somebody get to the airport quick . . . the bear was chewing his way out of the crate. I grabbed an assistant, jumped into the truck, and arrived at the airport in less than forty minutes.

The air-freight terminal was completely locked; all work had ceased. We saw one man start to wave his arms frantically when he saw the zoo truck. His first words were, "Quickly, quickly!" I grabbed the tranquilizing equipment and followed him into a side door. It led to an office where ten men were peering through a small window at a lone baggage cart in the middle of the massive air-freight building. The cart was rocking back and forth in the dim confines of the building. When my eyes focused, I saw the bear. He had one leg and one shoulder out of the crate. I could see him chewing small chunks of the crate and spitting them onto the baggage cart. He would be out in ten minutes. I loaded a syringe with an adequate dose of phencyclidine hydrochloride, walked into the terminal, and climbed onto the baggage cart. The bear—not a mean bear—looked at me as if to say, "Could you help me get out of here?" I gave him a quick shot in the shoulder, and he never even winced. He quickly fell asleep. The workers at air freight cheered, and after a quick look at the creature that had brought their world to a halt, they returned to work sadly behind schedule.

We loaded the bear and the demolished crate onto the truck and returned to the zoo. When we arrived we were met by the curator and a host of keepers who were getting a good laugh out of the whole incident. The bear was carried to his grotto while the curator fingered the shredded plywood and torn aluminum. Our eyes met briefly. I was hoping she would say something—anything—that would help me feel comfortable in her presence. She stormed off. But you could have sent an elephant in the next crate she had built.

I never learned to enjoy her company and have always taken more pleasure in that incident than I should. However, I did learn something from her. My father-in-law said it best: "Everyone is good for something if only to serve as a bad example." I learned again how poor it is to treat people like dirt, to make them feel small and inadequate.

C. S. Lewis writes in *Mere Christianity:*

> In God you come up against something which is in every respect immeasurably superior to yourself. Unless you know God as that—and, therefore, know yourself as nothing in comparison—you do not know God at all. As long as you are proud you cannot know God. A proud man is always looking down on things and people: and, of course, as long as you are looking down, you cannot see something that is above you.
>
> Luckily, we have a test. Whenever we find that our religious life is making us feel that we are good—above all, that we are better than someone else—I think we may be sure that we are being acted on, not by God, but by the devil. The real test of being in the presence of God is that you either forget about yourself altogether or see yourself as a small, dirty object. It is better to forget about yourself altogether.

Good for Something

Aren't you glad Jesus is no respecter of persons?

For all have sinned and come short of God's glory.

Romans 3:23

The Lord is not slow about His promise, as some count slowness, but is patient toward you, not wishing for any to perish but for all to come to repentance.

2 Peter 3:9

Cherish the
Butterflies

It's sad, but it's true. The earth is dying. It is wearing out.
The Bible said it was going to, but until our generation I
believe nobody took these passages seriously. But they are
there and very plain to see if you have eyes to see. Let me
show you.

Psalms 102:26 tells us that the earth will "wear out
like a garment." Revelation 11:18 warns that the time will
come ". . . for destroying the destroyers of the earth."
Isaiah the prophet saw what would happen the most
clearly, and he even knew who would cause it. The scene is
earth and the final demise of Satan. There are people
standing around the edge of a great pit. They are looking
at Satan and saying, "Is this the man who made the earth
tremble, who shook kingdoms, who made the world like a
desert?" Like a desert—barren, lacking fresh water, and
devoid of abundant life. Does it seem possible that our

world, whose land mass is 75 percent forest, could become a desert? Fifty years ago that scripture would have been offered as a symbolic overstatement. But not anymore.

Isaiah further amplifies in 10:19, "The remnant of the trees of his forest will be so few that a child can write them down." What kind of numbers can a child conceive? Ten, maybe twenty. When Satan is cast into the pit the trees have something to say. "The cypresses rejoice at you, the cedars of Lebanon, saying, 'Since you were laid low, no hewer (woodcutter) comes up against us'" (Isaiah 14:18).

Let us consider the history of Israel. G. S. Cansdale, in his wonderful book *All the Animals of Bible Lands,* states, "Man has left his mark all over the world, but the lands of the Bible have been occupied and used since the birth of civilization, so it is not surprising that he has done more damage there than almost anywhere else, leaving great areas of soil impoverished or even eroded down to bare rock. This is reflected in the flora, poor in species and poor on the ground and this in turn in the fauna." When Abraham came to the Promised Land it was a woodland. His only source of fuel was wood, so he and those after him began to cut down the trees and clear the land. Because of wars the land was often salted so that nothing would grow for long periods of time. It began as a land flowing with milk and honey but it became an ecological nightmare.

Satan has been busy throughout history at the task of destroying the earth, but it seems to have become a higher priority in our age of technology. All the world is following the pattern of Israel. In Southern California one out of eight trees is dying because of our air pollution. But we are better off than the eastern United States. The auto and steel industries are belching millions of tons of sulphur dioxide into the atmosphere. Rain clouds pick it up and redistribute it all over the East Coast and Canada. Oak trees are dying by the thousands, and whole forests are being stunted. Fish are becoming unable to reproduce because of metal build-ups caused by the acid rains. Robert

H. Boyle writes in his sobering book, *Acid Rain,* that we are absolutely devastating Canada with our toxic emissions. The effects of acid rain originating in the eastern U. S. to date include killing all the fish in 1,200 lakes; 3,400 are nearly dead; 11,400 are at risk; and in twenty years 48,500 lakes are likely to lose their fish.

Germany is even further down the road. One out of three trees in their famous Black Forest is dying because of smog damage. Pollution is not the only problem that the trees are experiencing. Direct cutting in South America is taking one acre of forest every 1.2 seconds—that's 50 acres per minute, or 42,000 square miles a year. These facts were gleaned from Paul and Anne Ehrlich's powerful book, *Extinction.*

Did you know that more than three million acres are paved over every year? Isaiah 5:8 says, "Woe to those who join house to house, who add field to field, until there is no more room." Satan's desert may not be as far into the future as we would like to believe. He is not in "the pit" yet, and he is actively working at the destruction of the earth.

What does Satan get out of all this? A chance to kill many people. The trees filter pollution out of the air and they exchange carbon dioxide for oxygen. They also liberate millions of gallons of water into the atmosphere. The water becomes rain. We need those trees. Satan knows all this, but he is now and has always been a murderer. What an effective way of killing millions. Africa is already experiencing the beginning of the ecological end. Their famines are the result of poor land management and a total disregard for the ecological balance.

Isaiah saw it all. "The earth mourns and withers. . . . The earth lies polluted under its inhabitants. . . . The earth is utterly broken, the earth is rent asunder, the earth is violently shaken" (24:4–5, 19). Isaiah was given a look at what the future of the earth would include. As he wrote, he was accounting for events that would not occur for 2,700 years. He saw our now, and it's happening just as he said it would. He saw the effects; we know the causes. Decimation of species, chemical pollution, destruction of habitat, and overuse—these are the weapons we have used to destroy the earth.

How do you think God feels about the way we are treating His magnificent creation? Not good, I think. Dante said, "Nature is the art of God." We are defacing His art. His art is functional art. It takes care of us.

Think about John Drinkwater's poetry:

> When you defile the pleasant streams,
> And the wild birds' abiding place.
> You massacre a million dreams,
> And cast your spittle in God's face.

Why is God putting up with our meaningless and futile defacement of His priceless work of art? I believe there is a complete explanation nestled in the middle of Romans 8:19–20:

> For the creation waits with eager longing for the revealing of the sons of God; for the creation was subjected to futility, not of its own will but by the will of him who subjected it in hope. . . .

Let me paraphrase the above verses. I think you will be moved by what God's spirit has revealed through the apostle Paul.

All of nature is awaiting with enthusiasm and deep longing for everyone who is going to come to the Lord to do so. God has ordered nature to put up with man's needless abuse. Nature didn't want to, but God ordered nature to take man's abuse to give man more time to come to Him. If you want to get a concrete picture of what this verse is saying, consider this illustration.

Michelangelo is in his studio. Around the room are several of his most cherished masterpieces. His love and greatest skills are evident in every stroke of the brush

82

Cherish the Butterflies

and cut of the chisel. His work praises his genius and expresses his deepest thoughts. Suddenly, a servant boy that he loves dearly throws open the studio door. It is evident that he is severely mentally disturbed. He doesn't comprehend the love of the master artist and is, in fact, needlessly jealous of his abilities and authority. The servant boy rushes forward and slashes many of the paintings and dashes many of the sculptures to the floor. Much of the art is beyond repair and lost forever. Michelangelo walks to the servant boy and holds him in a long embrace. He then speaks softly, "My boy, you mean more to me than the art. I want you to be my son. We can work this out." Michelangelo shares with the other servants that for now the boy is not to be punished. The boy will be given more time to be willing for adoption. The servants express their anger and shock at what has happened but they promise to stand with the master's choice.

Our Father never misses a sparrow's fall. The fact that He has not destroyed us for what we have done to His beautiful creation is all the assurance we should ever need of His love.

May I give you more of an idea of what it means for the creation to have been subjected to futility? We need only to look to what has happened to our own ecology in the United States to get an idea of the needless pain that nature has suffered on our behalf.

The American bison knows of the futility of man. When our forefathers set foot on this continent they found that it was teeming with life. There were turkeys to be shot so that the early colonists could make it through that first severe winter. There were hooved animals on every hillside and in every valley. Fish were teeming in every sparkling stream. One animal dominated the scene and provided meat and hide in generous abundance. That was the American bison. When the pilgrims stepped onto Plymouth Rock, it is estimated that North America sustained a population of seventy-five million of the impressive hooved Goliaths.

83

The North American Indians killed only what they needed. And throughout the 1700's there were not enough settlers to pose a threat to the bisons' existence.

All this wonderful balance began to erode by 1810. A European market developed for meat and hides, and buffalo hunting began in earnest. Names like Buffalo Bill Cody, Kit Carson, and Jim Bridger became household words. They were the great white hunters of our continent and their time. By 1832 the last buffalo east of the Mississippi was killed. David A. Dary says all this in his great book *The Buffalo Book: The Saga of an American Symbol.*

Hunting became a sport and people were encouraged to shoot the buffalo from trains as they journeyed westward. No thought was given to whether they might be wasting a valuable resource or whether they just wounded or actually killed the beasts they shot from the moving trains.

When the United States government realized how dependent the Indians were on the bison, they encouraged eradication of the species. The Indians could be relegated to reservations more easily if they were starving and cold.

By 1895 there were less then 400 buffalo in existence. We killed almost the total population of 75 million in 85 years.

There were other casualties of the westward movement. As we settled the West we killed the wolves, both the red and grey. There are about 1,600 left in the wild. There used to be more than a million.

The largest bird in North America, the condor, suffered an indirect slaughter. They were carrion eaters, and we had wasted their food supply. God had designed them to eat dead animals, especially dead bison. They were His clean-up crew. But so much of their food had been eradicated that they began to starve to death. When America was first settled, there were close to one and a half million condors. Now there are a mere 26 struggling to hold on to their existence. All of them are in captivity. Their only hope is for an artificial breeding breakthrough. They have long since passed the point when they could recover on their own.

Our American symbol, the bald eagle, has not fared too well, either. We have less than one-tenth of the original population. Insecticides and destruction of habitat took them.

Think about the demise of the great whales. Farley Mowat in his moving account, *A Whale for the Killing*, shows the decline of the whale population between the years of 1930 and 1972. Some species which had been in the hundreds of thousands have dropped 75, 80, even 90 percent. The grey whale is extinct altogether, and the right whale and the blue whale are on the brink of extinction.

Whales are fantastic animals. They have I.Q.'s that rival mankind's. They cooperate with each other in hunting, they care for each other when they get sick, and they sing songs that can be heard by other whales more than thirty miles away. They have been quietly tolerant of man's abuse to their species. They have remained subject to the futility of man as God had decreed.

And they have suffered. The statistics reveal the decline of the whales, but they do not demonstrate the agony they have endured. The principal method of killing whales has always been harpooning. The sensitive animals were repeatedly harpooned and forced to drag boats for miles as they tried to keep up with their family groups. When they became too exhausted to swim any farther, the whalers would spear them over and over until loss of blood slowly but surely claimed their lives. This is a warm-blooded animal that nurses its young and loves its family.

One of the most sickening facts to surface in recent years involves our U. S. Navy. Farley Mowat records the incident in *A Whale for the Killing*.

> Until after the Second World War there were almost no sightings of great whales off the south coast of

Newfoundland. Then, in the late 1940's, U.S. Naval air-craft flying out of the leased base at Argentina in southwest Newfoundland began spotting an occasional big whale. News of these sightings came to light in the mid-1950's when it was learned that whales had become a useful addition to the Navy's antisubmarine training. Aircraft crews, engaged in practice patrol work, had been instructed to pretend that any whales they spotted were Russian submarines. The whales became targets for cannon fire, rockets, bombs and depth charges!

In 1957 an outcry by Harold Horwood, a crusading columnist on the *St. John's Evening Telegram*, resulted in a promise from the Argentina officials that whales would no longer be used as targets.

The number either killed, wounded, or attacked over a ten-year period was never released. Presumably, it was classified information.

I could go on and on until you were overloaded with facts, statistics, and stories of man's inhumanity to the animal kingdom. I could tell you that there are less than two hundred and fifty grizzly bears left in the United States. I could tell you that until they became protected, the mountain lion was hunted almost to extinction. If I were to include worldwide statistics, you would discover that in your lifetime you may expect to hear about the passing out of existence of the following animals: mountain gorillas, cheetahs, African elephants, rhinos, and thousands of other lesser-known species.

At the present rate of extinction, we will be losing one-fifth of the world's species by the end of this century. There are times that I wish the animals would fight back. They could, you know. There are enough bees or bacteria to kill every man, woman, and child on the earth. But they won't, because they have been subjected.

There may be no greater example of God's patience with man than His putting up with man's abuse of His

great creation. Remember that this is all to give time for
people to come to the Lord Jesus Christ.

I agree with Andre Crouch: "I don't know why Jesus
loves me but I'm glad, so glad He did." Our proper response to His great love is to share it. We should be bringing people to Jesus.

I've told you the bad news. Now let me tell you the
good news. In fact, this earth will pass away, as will the
present heaven, but the Lord will make new ones. They will
be far better creations and they will be populated with
perfect, sinless, and forgiven people. He will set His children on a cloud somewhere in eternity and speak these new
creations into existence. You and I may be there to see it.
The Scripture says that the new earth will have neither sun
nor moon, for it will be illuminated by the glory of the Lord
Himself. The seas will be no more, but no one will be disappointed. This just means that there will be lakefront property for everyone. Lots of eagles, I bet, filling crystal-clear
skies. Did I tell you about the animals? They will all be
tame. If you want to hug a lion, no problem. If you want to
pick up a cobra, go ahead. Consider these verses from the
Book of Isaiah:

The wolf shall dwell with the lamb,
   and the leopard shall lie down with the kid,
and the calf and the lion and the fatling together,
   and a little child shall lead them.
The cow and the bear shall feed;
   their young shall lie down together;
   and the lion shall eat straw like the ox.
The suckling child shall play over the hole of the asp,
   and the weaned child shall put his hand on the adder's den.
They shall not hurt or destroy
   in all my holy mountain;
for the earth shall be full of the knowledge of the LORD
   as the waters cover the sea.

Isaiah 11:6–9

If you think that sounds great, then enjoy what the apostle Paul shares with us in 1 Corinthians 2:9:

> . . . no eye has seen, nor ear heard,
> nor the heart of man conceived,
> what God has prepared for those who love him.

We only see a small band of the colors that exist in the universe, just those of the rainbow. They are beautiful, but we haven't seen anything yet. Moths see a whole spectrum of colors we have never seen, but will.

We hear in a small band of the sounds that exist. Foxes hear a far wider range than we do. We are thrilled to hear orchestras and choirs play in eight octaves, but just wait for the thrill of hearing angel choirs burst forth in eighty octaves. Our music will have sounded so incomplete.

Go ahead. Push the limits of your imagination. Try and picture wonders far beyond any you have ever known. Well, God is planning things immeasurably better than you have just imagined. Don't you love God for that? If you don't, won't you try? You just won't want to miss out on the future that He has planned for those that love Him.

Mrs. Bedlam

The keepers at the Los Angeles Zoo had a saying: "The zoo would be a great place to work if you could just keep the people out." Like any saying, it had a background. Allow me to illustrate.

You would think you could trust senior citizens to behave themselves at the zoo. They were normally our most cherished visitors. But one little old lady engineered a mission of mercy that created more bedlam than any single visitor in the zoo's history. She looked innocent enough. She wore a faded black dress under her full-length black wool coat, and she displayed a wide-brimmed black hat with a silk rose that looked like it had been run over by a bus. But somehow, she passed security and the ticket-takers with two shopping bags filled to the brim with rubber balls. They were all shapes, colors, sizes, and textures.

She had been to the zoo many times before and had

concluded the animals were bored. In her mind, she was carrying two bags of recreation.

She threw a ball into the sea lion pool, and I'm sure she felt affirmed as the most playful animal of the zoo pushed it back and forth. She threw them into the bear moats, and the bears ate them, as did the monkeys. We knew that because the rubber showed up undigested in their waste material. Many of the animals simply ignored them, but not our female black-maned lioness. The ball thrown into her moated area was made of a very hard, dark blue rubber. The lioness bit down on it so hard that it was impaled on her awesome right canine. No amount of clawing at the ball dislodged it, and the female became increasingly distressed. She rubbed her face on the ground hoping to drag it loose. Her muzzle began to drip blood and mud, and she was salivating profusely. The keeper knew his animal needed help, and he called the health center and begged us to come quickly. His lioness was in trouble.

Dr. Bradford was the veterinarian on duty. He was brand new—just out of school. He had never worked with a lion before. Upon arriving we noticed the keeper had managed to lock the lioness in her night quarters. Dr. Bradford leaned on the bars to get a better look at her problem. She hated people and never tolerated anyone touching her cage. Knowing this, I reached out to pull him away, but it was too late. She lunged at his face and roared. Now a roar under any circumstance is impressive; but inside a small, concrete building, it is a major event. It rumbled through our bodies like thunder and we found ourselves momentarily paralyzed—and we were expecting it. Our young veterinarian wasn't expecting it, so he fainted. He lay on the cement floor for a few seconds. When he had again become coherent, he said something I will not quote in case children are reading this. The essence of his comment was that he now believed in lions.

I think he enjoyed shooting the lioness with the tranquilizer gun and would have enjoyed shooting the little old lady more, but we never saw her again. She did call the next day, though, to see if the animals enjoyed the rubber balls. When she was told how we had to remove the rubber ball with a hacksaw, she hung up.

I think we all understood that her motives were pure, but she clearly demonstrated a human potential. She did the wrong thing for the right reason. She was sincere, but she was sincerely wrong. The effect was the same as doing the wrong thing for the wrong reason. She could not have caused any more trouble if she had intended to harm the lioness.

Her major problem was that she was acting beyond her sphere of authority. She had no permission to act at all. She took this matter into her own hands.

This is when we create the most problems for ourselves —when we take matters into our own hands and act outside of God's authority. Intentions don't cut it. You've heard the old cliché, "The road to hell is paved with good intentions."

Dietrich Bonhoeffer, in his book *Ethics*, makes an interesting observation: "The tree of knowledge of Good and Evil produced the ability to choose our own good or our own evil." Both choices may take us an equal distance from God. But we have a third alternative—God's will.

One of my favorite films is "The Sound of Music." My favorite moment in the film is when Mother Superior asks Maria, "What is the most important thing you have learned at the abbey?" Maria humbly answers, "To find God's will and do it." God has given us His Word for a lamp to light the way. His will is not hidden. And His Scripture provides all the authority we need to act rightly.

David wrote, "I have laid up thy word in my heart, that I might not sin against thee" (Ps. 119:11). He learned to do that after feeling the full effects of taking matters into his own hands.

Stop and think about your life. Do you have permission to be living the way you are? If you are not sure, find out. If you don't, stop whatever you are doing right now . . . before you get hurt or you hurt someone else.

Pharmakia

I don't remember his name, but I will never forget his face. If I live to be one hundred, even five hundred, I will not forget. That is all I have ever seen of this young man, his face—actually, just a picture of his face. It was grainy, black and white, and on the front page of the *Los Angeles Times*. It captured a human being's last few seconds of conscious existence.

The photograph framed a man on his hands and knees crawling out of a pool at the Melbourne Zoo in Australia. His face was turned towards the camera but his eyes were turned upward, trying to glimpse the massive polar bear in whose jaws his head was firmly fixed. His eyes were so sad and revealed a mixture of terror, confusion, surprise, and pain. The corners of his mouth were turned down the way they might be just before a huge sob. How could this happen? And why would anybody want to capture this moment of horror on film?

It made an extra large impression on me because, at the time the picture was taken, I was taking care of our zoo's polar bear, Ivan. Ivan was a likely mankiller, and I had suffered many dreams in which I was the man in the photograph. Polar bears are one of the few animals that will hunt man as prey on a normal basis. They may be the animal most feared by zoo personnel in general.

The article explained. It seems the man had taken a rather large dose of LSD. His friend explained that he had hoped that it would help him experience the animals at the zoo at a different level of consciousness. While gazing at the polar bears, he perceived that they wanted to be his friends. Before anyone could stop him, he dove into their pool and swan to greet them. The polar bears greeted him as any predator would greet its prey. The male polar bear was probably slightly confused. Making a kill was not usually this easy, and prey had never offered itself to be killed.

I wondered about the photograph as I examined it for a clue. Was the man's expression the sudden fleeting reflection of one who was aware that he had been lied to? Did he manage one last tragic look at the real world, the world from which he was trying to escape when he began his journey with mind-altering drugs?

This incident was not the only one of its kind. Something very much like it happened at the Los Angeles Zoo several years later. It happened, as far as anyone could tell, late on a weekday afternoon. No one saw it happen, but the evidence told the story so clearly that it read like a book.

The event announced itself suddenly, without warning. The time had come to close the zoo. It was fifteen minutes to five and time to let the animals in for the night. All over the zoo animals were anxiously awaiting the opportunity to receive the best portion of their food and sleep in their comfortable night quarters. Dave, the keeper who cared for the lions, had performed this ritual a thousand times before. The lions' night cages were clean and dry and several pounds of Zupreem Feline Diet were awaiting them. Dave gave a pull on the lever that lifted the guillotine door. It changed into position but no lions ran into the night cage. He looked into the opening created by the raised door and his heart stopped beating. There in the dim light was the female lioness. Her muzzle was bloody and she was snarling over her prey—a man, or what was left of a man. Dave gasped and ran for a phone.

When the investigation was concluded, the man's story was pieced together. This man has chosen phencyclidine hydrochloride to find another less painful plane of existence. Because this drug has so many different effects, it was impossible to determine what motive caused him to take a detour into a nightmare. No note, no friend, no clue as to why this man confronted our lioness in her territory. We were told that he had entered the exhibit by leaping to a palm tree that grew near the twenty-foot wall around the moated area. His arm must have shown the abrasions or his clothes must have disclosed fibers from the tree because the police were certain that this was the way he entered the exhibit.

There was no way of knowing just how the next moments passed. I don't want to know. His death may have been mercifully quick, for no human came forward who had heard him cry out. He must have been sadly alone, with no one present who cared.

One of our keepers lost his fingers to a hyena named Hatari. Hatari had been used in the John Wayne movie of the same name. This keeper, while under the influence of marijuana, lost two important qualities necessary for working around wild animals. He lost his good judgment and his timing. While trying to do his job after a brief encounter with a marijuana joint, he stumbled and grabbed for the chain link fence to keep from falling. Hatari was only too glad to take his fingers.

Drugs, more properly called pharmaceuticals, derive their name from the Greek word *pharmakia*. Whenever this word is translated in the Bible it is rendered sorcery. It was understood to be the devil's work. And so it has become in our age. It's just like the devil to take a wonderful life-saving science like pharmacology and turn it into the number one killer of our youth. Suicide by overdose claims more of our youth than any other single cause of death. In the Book of John, verse 44 of chapter 8, we read about Satan's method of operation. It tells us that Satan is a liar and a murderer and he has been so from the beginning.

Whenever I remember these stories I think of them as prime victories for the enemy. I am as sure as I can be that drug abuse is our nation's number one problem. It is tearing our youth to pieces.

Be sober, be watchful. Your adversary the devil prowls around like a roaring lion, seeking some one to devour. Resist him, firm in your faith . . . .

1 Peter 5:8–9

Perpetual Adolescents

There are two kinds of chimpanzees: those that let things happen and those that make things happen. Our zoo had both, and they both caused a pile of trouble.

Zoo chimps are bored. They really don't have enough to do and it makes them a little crazy most of the time.

Most of their time is spent waiting. They wait to be let out in the morning. They wait for enough food to get them through the day. They wait to be let in at night so that they can eat their fill and sleep till morning. They watch people watching them and sometimes they throw things at them (disgusting things). They fight a little and play a little, but mostly they wait.

So it's not surprising that the day they were offered an opportunity for diversion they took it. You see, one of the zoo patrons noticed that there was a fifty-foot long, one-inch hose neatly coiled right in front of the chimp exhibit.

He must have said to himself, "Self, if you throw that hose over the edge of the exhibit, it will provide an excellent escape ladder for the chimps." And that is exactly what he did.

He couldn't have realized the dangerous situation that he was creating for the public. Most of our chimps were very neurotic, and when they were out of the exhibit they could become quite excited. The adults were four to six times as strong as a man, and a good number of them had periods during which they were very aggressive for no apparent reason.

While the chimps were making their escape, I was counting the minutes until quitting time. That was not my usual practice, but then this was not a usual day. It was June 19th and it was my seventh wedding anniversary. My wife, Carol, would be looking good and my mouth was watering for prime rib. When the phone rang, I felt a twinge of fear that something was going to make me late for our celebration.

I couldn't have been more accurate. A security guard calmly informed us that eight chimpanzees were out of their moated area and mingling with the public. We grabbed our capture equipment and headed out.

When we arrived we were treated to the most frightening sight I have ever witnessed. Jeanie, a highly unpredictable and sometimes very aggressive female, was hovering over a baby stroller. Her mouth was wide open and her lethal teeth were resting against the skull of a three-month-old baby girl. Jeanie was not showing any signs of aggression, but that didn't mean that two seconds later she wouldn't be. The baby's mother looked concerned, but she didn't appear to be unduly frightened. I cautioned our new vet not to make any moves until Jeanie was clear of the baby. Some of the other chimps noticed me because I was in uniform, and they began to holler. Jeanie looked around, saw us, and took off running. All of the chimps knew we had a tranquilizer gun, and they began to back away. I called out to the zoo patrons that these chimps were very dangerous and told them to leave the area for their own safety. We wouldn't attempt any capture activity until they were safely out of sight.

When we finally exposed the tranquilizer gun, a very funny thing happened. Toto, our oldest and largest male, led three of the females back to the hose and climbed back into the exhibit. This group huddled together and patted each other. That's what chimps do to comfort each other when they are very upset.

Other keepers began to arrive, and two of the babies recognized them and crawled into their arms. They had sensed the fear in the parents and were in an emotional turmoil. But they calmed down quickly when the keepers carried them to the back of their exhibit.

Only two rebelled—the erratic Jeanie and the delicate Antoinette, more affectionately known as Annie. They climbed the guardrail and made their way deep into the landscaping between their own moat and the Indian rhino yard. Herman, the Indian rhino, was beside himself with rage. He charged and snorted and even reared up slightly hoping to get a chance to bash a chimp.

The growth between the two exhibits was dense and difficult to penetrate. It was a non-negotiable tangle of wild roses and ivy.

Our job was to get into a position to shoot a tranquilizer dart into Jeanie first in the hopes that Annie would surrender and climb back into the moat. Dr. Bradford felt that since he was paid the most, he should take the risk of shooting the angry chimp. I told him I thought he was right. He carried the rifle over the guardrail and I followed him with the pistol. That would be used for backup if the first shot missed. We spread the wild roses apart and saw our two escapees. They were huddled in the shadows and screamed their disapproval at our presence.

Dr. Bradford took careful aim and a blast of air propelled a dart swiftly to the generous hindquarters of the female chimpanzee.

Jeanie reacted instantly, but not the way we had hoped. She charged screaming with anger, her teeth showing from ear to ear.

I knew that as soon as she saw the pistol she would stop and run away, but Dr. Bradford didn't know that, so he made a run for it. He was a big man, and when he turned to run he knocked me flat. The pistol went flying. Dr. Bradford tripped over me and began to fall into the rhino moat. Herman, more enraged than ever, was trying his best to horn the doctor. As Dr. Bradford was falling I had grabbed one leg and was now holding on to him for dear life. I was sure Jeanie was going to be biting us any second so I had closed my eyes to concentrate on keeping the vet out of the rhino yard. She must have seen the pistol before it went flying and ceased her charge because we were never bitten.

With great effort, the doctor pulled himself back over the edge of the moat and breathlessly thanked me for grabbing him. We peered back into the undergrowth and saw Jeanie showing the effects of the powerful tranquilizer. As we has hoped, Annie jumped back into the exhibit by herself. And three minutes later Jeanie was asleep for the night.

Chimpanzees are perpetual adolescents, never quite ready to take the responsibility for the freedom they so desperately seem to want. Of all the great apes, they are the most playful and the least dignified. They are childlike. At the time of this writing, Toto is nearly fifty years of age and still totally irresponsible. In fact, from what I could gather, he is worse than ever. But it's okay because Toto is a chimp.

One of the fundamental differences between a man and a chimpanzee is that a man may choose to become responsible. If we are responsible we have opted for maturity. We have grown up. If we are possessed of all our faculties, growing up is what we are supposed to do. It is expected of us, and if we don't, someone, usually our parents, are disappointed and embarrassed.

The apostle Paul was disappointed with the church members at the city of Corinth. They never grew up. His words express his disappointment.

> But I, brethren, could not address you as spiritual men, but as men of the flesh, as babes in Christ. I fed you with milk, not solid food; for you were not ready for it; and even yet you are not ready, for you are still of the flesh. For while there is jealousy and strife among you, are you not of the flesh, and behaving like ordinary men?
>
> 1 Corinthians 3:1–3

It's not that they didn't have the knowledge that adults acquire, because they did. It's not that they didn't have the Spirit of God, because they did. They were babies because they couldn't take the responsibility for the freedom to serve and obey Christ. They wouldn't care for others. Like children and adolescents they simply focused on their own needs. But the mature in Christ focus on the needs of others.

The author of Hebrews directs his thoughts to the same issue: maturity.

> About this we have much to say which is hard to explain, since you have become dull of hearing. For though by this time you ought to be teachers, you need some one to teach you again the first principles of God's word. You need milk, not solid food; for every one who lives on milk is unskilled in the word of righteousness, for he is a child. But solid food is for the mature, for those who have their faculties trained by practice to distinguish good from evil.
>
> Hebrews 5:11–14

Maturity Test
1. On whose needs are you focused?
2. Are you consistent in doing the right thing?
3. Are you serving others?

If you have been a Christian for some time, I can say something to you I could never say to a chimp. "Don't you think it's time to grow up?" If you haven't been a Christian for some time, then you may need to know that the questions should have been answered like this: 1.) Others; 2.) Yes; 3.) Yes.

Practice what you learn in the faith as you learn it. In no time at all you will be maturing nicely.

Anybody for an

Elephant?

You never know what might happen when you do someone a favor. When an admiral of the United States Navy tried to help out the premier of Cambodia, it led to all sorts of trouble for the Los Angeles Zoo.

This is the shameful story. Only the names have been changed, as there is no further need to embarrass any of the irresponsible parties.

During the late 1960s and early 1970s Los Angeles was known to be the only city in the United States with its own foreign policy. Our mayor was out of town as often as possible nursing a delusion of grandeur and embracing thoughts of the presidency. He was always speaking on behalf of our Vietnam policy and making lots of friends in the military. It was one of those friendships that led to the Los Angeles Zoo being asked to accept a male elephant. The story the veterinarians and I received firsthand from the assistant director of the zoo was stranger than fiction.

The premier of Cambodia had become deathly ill and was in need of a delicate surgical process not available in his own country. The nearest help available was on an American aircraft carrier stationed off the coast of his embattled kingdom. So the navy flew him to the carrier and a team of expert surgeons saved his life.

The Cambodians had a strange way of saying thank you. A simple thank-you note would have been more than enough, but tradition is tradition and must be observed. The Cambodian tradition demanded that a male elephant be given to the man most responsible for the saving of another's life. And the premier decided that the admiral directing the fleet operations from the aircraft carrier was the man deserving of the honor.

Now the admiral was the epitome of a crusty old salt. He had a raspy voice, short white hair, and skin wrinkled and blotched from thousands of hours of chafing wind, salt spray, and reflected sun from all the seas of the world. He was just the kind of man who didn't need an elephant. But it would be an unforgivable breach of protocol to refuse a gift of such magnitude. So in the style of a man who has learned to survive wars and presidents, he acknowledged the offer and began making plans to accept the elephant. I'll bet you're thinking, "What's the problem? A free elephant sounds like a pretty great deal, right?" Wrong.

The problem is that the elephant was a male. Male elephants are dangerous. They resist training and become unmanageable at various times during the year. After many deaths of keepers and trainers, zoos throughout the world have decided to keep only females.

When the admiral called the mayor we assume the conversation must have proceeded something like this.

"Mayor, it's the admiral. Your city has a fine zoo I'm told."

"Yes, Admiral, I practically built it myself."

"The wife and I have come by a little gift and we would like to donate it to your zoo."

"Sounds great, Admiral. What is it?"

"It's a male elephant, Mayor."

"Sounds like a generous gift. Let me call our people at the zoo and make the arrangements."

So the mayor called the zoo. We *know* how the conversation went on our end.

"Mayor, we really can't accept the male elephant. It's just too dangerous. That animal would hurt somebody out here. You could count on it, Your Honor."

The mayor took the news reluctantly and phoned the hopeful admiral to break the bad news. At this point we can only speculate on the pressure that was exerted on the mayor. Anyway, the mayor called back our way and addressed our director in the following manner.

"I would consider it a personal favor if you would provide a home for the admiral's elephant. It will require that you send some of your staff to Cambodia to pick it up. The navy will pick up the tab, and your people will go first class. I trust you'll have everything arranged at the zoo so that we can say thank you for the admiral's generous gift. By the way, the admiral's wife has made a small request. She would like the tusks as a souvenir. I trust you will work that out also. I really do appreciate your cooperation in this opportunity to help our country."

It would be impossible to refuse to do the mayor a personal favor, so our director "Yes, Your Honored" him half to death and agreed to care for a male elephant. He was met with a lot of resistance by the staff, but no one wanted to call the mayor back so a date was fixed. A team was sent to the other side of the earth to receive an expensive gift. Expensive for us, that is. It was to cost America more than three hundred thousand dollars just to accept the elephant.

To tell you the truth, there were a number of us that

would have loved to go to Cambodia, and we were disappointed when only one keeper was chosen. The director and the head administrator of the Los Angeles Zoo Association went to handle the protocol and make the necessary arrangements. A crate would need to be built and preparations for the extensive flight would need to be made.

Our clever director had the enormous crate built out of teak, tons of it, all of which was to become his when the elephant was unloaded at the Los Angeles Zoo.

The group was gone for two weeks, and the zoo was abuzz with gossip and speculation concerning the male elephant. Every keeper was sure that they would have told the mayor where to get off, but theirs was breaktime bravery. We all would have done what the director did. Still, breaktime was the only opportunity we got to direct the zoo, and we tried to make the best of it.

The return was well attended by those who anticipated a raging bull elephant. The crate was a good deal smaller than expected, and although it was teak, it was unfinished and no one suspected that it had any value at all. So much for the director's clever plan. When the door was swung open, the keeper who had been flown to Cambodia led the elephant out of the crate.

He was the most pitiful specimen we had ever seen. He was suffering from malnutrition and was clearly depressed. His eyes lacked luster, and even walking was an effort.

We were told that the little male's name was Chameroun (Sham-ah-roon), which means "prosperity" in Cambodian. If this poor excuse for an Asian elephant was their idea of prosperity, we were being given a graphic display of how depleted their nation had become.

As the veterinarian and I began the examination, we discovered one thing after another that would require extensive treatment. Chameroun was filled with internal parasites, which explained his poor condition. He would have to be isolated from the other elephants for weeks while he

Anybody for an Elephant?

was being treated. He also had suspicious looking lumps all over his body, which turned out to be another type of worm that burrows under the skin. Each worm would need to be removed surgically. It was a process that would take hours and hours.

Chameroun was too weak to be tranquilized, so the removing of his tusks for the admiral's wife would have to wait until his condition improved dramatically.

As time passed, Chameroun did improve. But as he improved he became less docile. It was clear that it would only be a matter of time until somebody got hurt. No one can stop an angry elephant from doing harm if harm is what it wants to do.

The official day to say thank you to the premier of Cambodia and the admiral came with pomp and pageantry. The zoo director thanked the mayor for the contact that led to the procurement of this rarely exhibited animal. The mayor thanked the admiral and his wife for thinking of Los Angeles when it came time to find a home for the generous gift, and he thanked America for giving him an opportunity to serve his world. Cambodian officials again thanked the admiral for saving their beloved premier.

I never expect to see that many liars plying their trade in one location again. No greater invitation for lightning has ever been issued unanswered.

The best thing that happened that day was a visit by the beautiful actress Candice Bergen. She was there gathering information for an uncomplimentary article that she was writing about the mayor. The article was entitled, "The Man in the Empty Suit." Several keepers were only too glad to explain how the mayor's pressure on the zoo to accept the elephant was sure to lead to the injury or even death of anyone responsible for its care.

The keepers were prophetic. An incident did occur which could have been fatal. A keeper sustained a severe back injury from Chameroun, and plans were made to remove the elephant from the collection. After two years, the

now healthy but unpredictable male was donated to a zoo in Mexico. As far as I know, that is where he is today.

As I thought through this story, I found three lessons that begged to be taught. First, there were many times for people to say no. The admiral could have refused to take the elephant, and in so doing saved the United States government three hundred thousand dollars. The mayor could have refused the admiral's offer when he discovered the danger factor in order to protect the keepers. The director could have said no on general principles and stood by the men that he was responsible to protect. Learning when to say no to situations that have no value or are counterproductive divide wise men from fools. But this story owned no wise men.

Second, we are never bound to obey anybody else's traditions. Dr. Charles Sedgwick, our greatest veterinarian, once told me—and I quote—"Gary, always be loyal to your own principles and you'll never have to worry whom to be loyal to." We only have to listen to the Scripture and our own conscience. Any other voices need not apply.

Third, we need to know that there are unexpected costs when we go out of our way to help others. By saving the premier's life, the admiral chose to be a Good Samaritan.

If we choose to play the role of the Good Samaritan, and we should, it is sure to cost us more than we will first anticipate. Do you remember the story of the Good Samaritan? It is found in Luke 10:25–37.

And behold, a certain lawyer stood up and put him to the test, saying, "Teacher, what shall I do to inherit eternal life?" And He said to him, "What is written in the Law? How does it read to you?" And he answered and said, "You shall love the Lord your God with all your heart, and with all your soul, and with all your strength, and with all your mind; and your neighbor as yourself." And He said to him,

Anybody for an Elephant?

"You have answered correctly; do this, and you will live."
But wishing to justify himself, he said to Jesus, "And who is
my neighbor?" Jesus replied and said, "A certain man was
going down from Jerusalem to Jericho; and he fell among
robbers, and they stripped him and beat him, and went off
leaving him half dead. And by chance a certain priest was
going down on that road, and when he saw him, he passed
by on the other side. And likewise a Levite also, when he
came to the place and saw him, passed by on the other side.
But a certain Samaritan, who was on a journey, came upon
him; and when he saw him, he felt compassion, and came to
him, and bandaged up his wounds, pouring oil and wine on
them; and he put him on his own beast, and brought him to
an inn, and took care of him. And on the next day he took
out two denarii and gave them to the innkeeper and said,
'Take care of him; and whatever more you spend, when I
return, I will repay you.' Which of these three do you think
proved to be a neighbor to the man who fell into the robbers' hands?" And he said, "The one who showed mercy
toward him." And Jesus said to him, "Go and do the same."

The Good Samaritan was good because he went out of
his way. He even anticipated that the favor would cost
more than he had already paid. It cost him time, energy,
and money—and there isn't much more that we can give.

I have a close friend that tells a story of his youth.
Sonny was late to school and had chosen to hitchhike to get
there quicker. Fortunately, a benevolent old man pulled
over and picked him up. Sonny thanked him for his kindness and they made small talk as they motored down Wash-
ington Boulevard in Pasadena. Sonny broke into their
conversation and said, "You can let me off here, sir."

The old man looked to both sides of the street and said
in a confused tone, "But I don't see any school, son."

"The school's a block up, sir; I can walk. I don't want
to take you out of your way."

The old gentleman spoke in a firm but kind way,
and said, "Son, when I stopped and picked you up a few

minutes ago, I set out to do you a favor. Now, if I don't go out of my way, I don't figure I've done you one."

Take a moment and think. When was the last time you went out of your way to do anybody a favor? What did it cost you? If you thought of something recent, thank the Lord. You're becoming more like Jesus. If you couldn't think of anything, don't stand around feeling guilty, go help somebody. Needy folks are all around us.

It Will Be

Different for Me

Bandit was irresistible. No raccoon that ever existed had more natural "cute" than this ninety-day-old bundle of mischief. When my neighbor Julie bought him at the pet store, she was sure they would be lifelong friends. Everywhere she went, he went—usually perched on her shoulder. Bandit's habit of holding Julie's cheeks in his paws and looking into her eyes with sparkling curiosity always melted her and solicited an affectionate kiss and hug. And he grew. Eighteen months passed and Bandit became a strapping twenty-five-pound adolescent raccoon, still full of the dickens and only slightly less playful. He still loved affection, rode on shoulders, and seemed to be a one-raccoon advertisement that raccoons make great pets.

I mentioned Julie and Bandit to our zoo veterinarian one day and inquired as to why more people didn't keep raccoons as pets. His answer floored me. "They undergo a glandular change at about twenty-four months. After that, they become unpredictable, independent, and often attack their owners."

"Are there exceptions?" I inquired.

"None that I know of," he said thoughtfully.

"Then Julie is likely to be bitten?"

"Any time now, I should think," the doctor added with conviction.

Since a thirty-pound raccoon can be equal to a one hundred-pound dog in a scrap, I felt compelled to mention the coming change to Julie. She sat and listened politely as I explained what an eminent world authority had shared with me concerning raccoons and their nature. I'll never forget her answer.

"It will be different for me . . . Bandit is different." And she smiled as she added, "Bandit wouldn't hurt me. He just wouldn't!"

Three months later, Julie underwent plastic surgery for facial lacerations sustained when her adult raccoon attacked her for no apparent reason. Bandit was released into the wild.

That happened about fifteen years ago, and I've heard Julie's reply many times since: "But it will be different for me."

Rob, a sixteen-year-old boy, said, "I know what I'm doing. It's different for me. I know all about dosages and stuff. My dad is a pharmacist." Rob overdosed six months later and spent two months in a mental ward.

Judy, a fifteen-year-old girl, argued, "I know he's been around, but it's different with us. He really loves me. He really does." Judy is now twenty-five and living at home with her nine-year-old son. The son never met his father.

Jerry, an eighteen-year-old college student, declared, "I'm different. A few drinks don't slow me down a bit." Jerry is dead now, and he took three friends with him when he drove off an embankment. They were all drunk.

Pat, a thirty-five-year-old woman, contended, "My kids are different. They will be able to handle the divorce fine. I'll spend more time with them. Besides, my lover is great with kids." Pat divorced her husband and got remarried to her lover. She divorced again after he tried to kill her. The children haven't slept well for years and need to see a counselor weekly.

David, a forty-plus-year-old executive, reasoned, "Wow, she's beautiful! Her husband is away on a business trip. Nobody will know. It will be different, exciting, temporary." David ended up causing this man's wife to be pregnant. To avoid scandal, he had the man killed. He felt compelled to marry the woman; then her baby died. David's life was never the same again. That incident caused members of his family to turn against him, and one of his children even tried to kill him. I'm sure he never dreamed that things would get so tangled. I'm sure he thought, "It will be different for me." (You can find this executive's biography beginning in 2 Samuel 11.)

Let's take one step back and look at our lives. Are we in violation of some well-known axiom? Are our closest friends or relatives warning us about something? Are we in conflict with the clear teaching of the Scriptures?

Now, repeat out loud the following phrase, "Maybe it won't be different for me."

The Theme
Building

The zoo was opened in September of 1966. It began its
marbled history as the world's fifth largest zoo and is the
only zoo in modern history that was actually opened as a
major zoo. In addition, it had several distinctions. First, we
accumulated more rare and endangered animals than any
other zoo in the world. And second, by the end of our third
year 52 percent of our collection was breeding annually.
Those two statistics were very prized in the zoo world and
commanded an early respect. But they also engendered a
fair amount of jealousy.

There were many criticisms of the Los Angeles Zoo
when it was first built. Some were justified and some were
not. For starters, it was built on a golf course which had
produced a fair amount of revenue for the city, whereas
the zoo lost a bundle every year. Also, the newly planted
grounds made it look like a desert. During the first

summers the sun fried anybody foolish enough to come without some sort of shade, and visitors were blinded by the stark grey exhibits wherever they went. It was often accused of being a concrete jungle. And it was.

The zoo was often criticized for its lack of showmanship as well. The supervisors resented presenting animals in acts of any kind. Their philosophy was that a zoo was an educational institution and ought not to pander to man's baser desires to be entertained when he ought to be educated.

The zoo was divided into nine sections: North America, South America, Africa, Australia, and Eurasia. Then there were the specialty sections: aquatics, birds, reptiles, and the children's petting zoo and nursery. The public rejected this arrangement at first because it made seeing their favorite type of animal more difficult. If you liked monkeys for instance, you would have to visit Africa, Eurasia, and South America to see them all, and in so doing you would have seen a number of animals you didn't want to see.

In the middle of the zoo stands its most prominent architectural feature—the Theme Building. It is placed on a rise that overlooks a fair portion of the main zoo, and its twin spires ascend ten stories into the sky. It is African, Indian, and Asian in appearance and really does set the architectural mood for the rest of the zoo. It's called the Theme Building, but what it really turned out to be was an extremely expensive roof with a dirt floor. You see, the committee that worked with the architect could not agree on what should go under the magnificent roof. The architect was able to convince them that they could decide later what should be built underneath it. As for now, he said, it set the theme and was too important to his concept to be left out. And so it was built.

As time passed, the debate raged on. Some thought the Theme Building should be turned into an expensive restaurant, others a gift shop, and some an educational center. Year followed year and all that the roof ever achieved was to provide shade for picnickers. Inexpensive benches were placed here and there under its ample eaves and zoo patrons simply ate lunches they had furnished for themselves.

The zoo has changed in hundreds of ways in the last twenty years. Waterfalls and expensive rock works are everywhere. The trees are tall and full and provide more than enough shade for the zoo patrons at any hour of the day. The animal collection is rare and beautiful, and not many people are complaining anymore. It is really a beautiful zoo, one of the very best. But you know what? The finest architectural monument at the zoo is still a million-dollar roof with a dirt floor. It hasn't changed at all. It stands empty after all these years. No one could decide what should go inside it, so empty it stays.

When I think about the Theme Building, it makes me wonder how many people go for twenty or thirty years without bringing something meaningful into their lives. The prophet Elijah spoke to his own people who could not decide who to bring into their lives. His speech may be found in 1 Kings 18:21.

> And Elijah came near to all the people, and said, "How long will you go limping with two different opinions? If the LORD is God follow him; but if Baal, then follow him." And the people did not answer him a word.

We were designed to be God's architectural wonder. We were made to be the temple of the Holy Spirit. Are you standing empty without His presence? Are you existing without anything inside? If you haven't before—let Him build your life into something meaningful.

Enter the Villain

It was early in the winter of 1968 when I was sent to the Los Angeles Zoo's version of Siberia. I had participated in the development of our local chapter of the American Association of Zoo Keepers, and most of our keepers were becoming involved in the organization. It was merely an educational fellowship, but our acting director was sure that it would become a labor union. He did everything he could to discourage our growth, and he even made attempts to control our activities. The group met after hours, off of zoo property, and we paid for our own speakers out of our own pockets.

One afternoon the director invited me to his office and told me what the organization could and could not print in our monthly newsletter. I was our group's vice president in charge of programming, and I made it clear that what we did on our own time with our own money was our concern and our concern only. I was insulted, and I told him that he had no more right directing our activities than those of the Boy Scouts of America. Our meeting came to an abrupt halt, and I was excused.

Two weeks later my supervisor came to me and said, "Richmond, I have bad news for you. You've been transferred to the 410 section."

The 410 section was reserved for those to be punished. It was larger than any section in the zoo and contained more animals than could be cared for in eight hours of work. I was sick for two reasons. One, I had known other keepers whose spirits had been broken by the immensity of the task. They were good men who had been drained of joy and heart. And two, I was very happy where I was.

I worked with Dr. Charles Sedgwick, the zoo's beloved veterinarian, caring for the animals at the health center. He was a thoughtful and considerate supervisor and was more than willing to spend every spare moment answering my endless string of questions. That time was the highlight of my zoo career. But it was now being ended by a man that I thoroughly disliked and had now begun to loathe.

I asked why I was being transferred, and the answer I was given was, "The acting director believes you have real potential and said it was time to broaden your horizons."

I was trained for two days on the 410 section, then I was left on my own. It didn't take me long to discover that I could not do the work in eight hours; it would take at least ten. I stayed an hour later each afternoon and worked through my break times so that I might have a nice-looking section. I even ate my lunch on the run, vowing that the acting director would not break my spirit. The energy that motivated me was the hatred that was growing in my soul. The section became a showcase, and I received satisfaction from the thought that the man might be bothered because I was doing the job. I was beating Siberia.

Then the rains came. It was the only year of my life

44

that it rained for eighteen consecutive days in Southern California. I had to move tons of dirt that had washed to the bottom of my exhibits back to the top. That was when my spirit began to die. The man who had done this to me would often drive by my section in his green Dodge Dart. I would gnash my teeth and get so angry that I would get an upset stomach. I entertained fantasies of the man dying in a fiery car crash. I even hoped the zoo's king cobra would bite him since I knew he could never survive. I hated him. I never thought about it. I just did.

It never occurred to me how my life was looking to others. I felt justified in my hatred. But I was to find out how I looked—the hard way.

My senior keeper's name was Scott. He confided in me one day that he was discouraged with life. He was drinking more than he thought he should, he was depressed, and he didn't feel any sense of purpose in life. I thought this a perfect time to share my faith in Christ.

"Have you ever thought about turning your life over to Christ?" I said in my most thoughtful and caring voice.

"Yeah," he said, "But I decided not to."

"Why?" I probed.

"Because all Christians are hypocrites."

"I'm a Christian and I'm not a hypocrite."

He smiled and said, "You are too." It was a disconcerting smile.

"Why do you say that?" I asked, hoping he didn't have a good reason.

"Aren't Christians supposed to love their enemies?"

"Yes."

"You hate the director's guts. I've seen you look at him like you want to kill him, and you bad-mouth him all the time. I'd say that is hypocrisy."

I was stunned. Everything he said was true. I sat there quietly for a moment trying to think of something clever to say, but nothing clever came. So I said, "You're right. I'm sorry I've been such a crummy example."

"You and everybody else," he said as he walked off.

I'm not sure that I have ever felt as ashamed as I did during that conversation. I asked the Lord's forgiveness and asked him to free me from the terrible hatred that had consumed my thoughts and directed my life. He did, because as 1 John 1:9 promises, "If we confess our sins, he is faithful and just, and will forgive our sins and cleanse us from all unrighteousness."

I was transferred from the 410 section a few weeks later when tears in the muscles of my lower abdomen made performing the task impossible. Eventually, I was transferred back to the health center and promoted to the same position that I was removed from several months before— you guessed it, by the acting director. We became friends.

Being confident of this very thing, that He who has begun a good work in you will perform it unto the day of Jesus Christ.

Philippians 1:6

What's It to You?

There was no doubt in my mind that my wife, Carol, was interested when I confessed that I was finding myself attracted to a twenty-four-year-old redhead named Sally. I shared that Sally was short, had beautiful brown eyes, was extremely affectionate, and was absolutely brilliant. I told her how Sally's auburn-red hair trailed gently down her back, arms, legs, and feet, and she even had some on her head. Carol was entertained when I admitted that Sally was an orangutan. Sally was under my care at the zoo's health center while her assigned mate, Eli, was being treated for tuberculosis in an adjacent cage.

Sally and Eli were as different as night and day. Sally was a butterball, sweet, helpful, gentle, and smart as a whip. Eli was grouchy, calculating, meaner than sin, and stronger than an ox.

Let me tell you some stories that will help you to know

them better. Now Sally was my favorite animal, and still is, so I will begin with her.

Any keepers worth their salt will offer their great apes something to do. In the wild these animals spend their time looking for food and shelter. Since those things are provided in a zoo, there is nothing for these intelligent and sensitive apes to do but watch an endless stream of people watching them. If you could imagine watching a movie which had no change of scenery, an everchanging cast, and no plot, then you have conceived what a great ape's existence might be like without a creative keeper. Lack of occupation leads to abnormal and aggressive behavior.

I loved to give Sally things to do because she always participated so enthusiastically. Problem solving was her forte. So I gave her lots to solve.

I would line up twenty peanuts exactly three feet out from the bars of her cage and give her a bath towel. Then Sally would fish for the peanuts by repeatedly casting the towel over them. Little by little she would drag them one at a time to the cage and place them in a neat little pile. She was so decent and orderly that I'm sure she was a Presbyterian.

I'll never forget the day of Sally's great discovery. I set up the peanuts in the normal fashion and handed her a white bath towel. She carefully unfolded it and draped it over her considerable lap, studying it thoughtfully. Then she gave me that "Eureka!" look. She got up quickly and scooted to her drinker, dragging the towel behind her. She looked back at me, and her expression told me she was onto something big. She dipped the towel in and out of the drinker several times until she was satisfied that it was thoroughly soaked. Then she wrung out the excess water. She ambled over to where I had placed the twenty peanuts and cast her wet towel over five of them. She retrieved them with just one effort. I was astounded. To tell you the truth, I'm not sure that I would have reasoned that a wet towel would have increased my advantage. But Sally did.

Sally viewed food as her great necessity. And you know what they say, "Necessity is the mother of invention."

Sally's love for food bordered on lust, and she developed whole routines to gain our empathy and attention. She would begin with lip smacking and graduate to body slapping. When we looked at her she would smile a gargantuan smile and point to her mouth. If nothing else worked she would croak forth with grunts and barking sounds that clearly displayed her frustration. One day she took a more direct approach.

I was passing by her cage to deliver a bunch of grapes to some primates at the back of the health center. Suddenly, Sally's mighty hand shot through the bars and grasped my arm with her iron grip. She gently but firmly pulled me close to the bars and pointed to the grapes. She smiled. There was no doubt in my mind that she wanted the grapes, and I found that a perfectly convenient time to let her have them. She took them in a most ladylike manner and delicately laid them on her sleeping bench. Keeping my arm firmly in her grasp, she reached out for the hand which had held the grapes, drew it slowly to her mouth, and kissed it. Then she patted me on the back as if to say, "Keep up the good work."

Sally was also helpful. She delighted in scraping up her leftover food into a neat pile and dropping it just outside her cage. On one morning I filled a bucket with warm soapy water and set it right next to her cage. I showed her how to clean the bars of her cage using a bath towel and then gave her the bath towel. She worked diligently for forty minutes scrubbing, rinsing, and wringing. She cleaned all the bars, her sleeping bench and her holding cage. That little effort won her a vanilla malt.

When Sally was finally allowed to be caged with Eli she became a prolific breeder. She is the mother of at least seven offspring. But her first birth was the most dramatic. Her baby Jonathan was born still encased in the placental sack. She had no idea that she needed to remove it, and we all watched in terror as she sat doing nothing while her newborn was dying for lack of oxygen. Finally, Dr. Sedgwick rushed in, at some personal risk, and took the baby. Nearly five minutes had passed before he tore the tiny orangutan from its birthing sack. The baby was cool, still, and hadn't taken a breath. He began CPR and stimulated the body with deliberate massage. Still no breathing or heartbeat. Dale Thompson, the keeper who was assisting Dr. Sedgwick, asked, "What do we do now?"

The heroic vet looked up long enough to say, "We don't give up. We never give up."

He injected a heart stimulant and the baby stiffened in response. All present cheered and then held their breath to see what would come of the doctor's last chance to retrieve the baby's ebbing life. The heartbeat was weak at first, and then it began to increase in volume and regularity. Jonathan would live. He will always be a little slow because of the severe oxygen deficit he suffered at birth, but he is alive and well and is bringing a great deal of pleasure to thousands of zoo visitors.

Sally is really something. Visitors to the Los Angeles Zoo still watch her perform her hilarious food routines. She has added a new gesture that I had never noticed while she was under my care. She uses her hand to shade her eyes from the glare of the sun.

Eli was nothing like Sally. He spent every waking moment looking for opportunities to pull keepers through the bars of his cage. We had to be watchful while walking near his cage because he had the kind of strength necessary to tear a man's arm off. A San Francisco zookeeper lost his arm to a large male orangutan during a careless moment.

I once saw Eli perform a feat of strength that made me a believer. Eli's cage was positioned next to a garage door that was opened every morning to ventilate the health center. When the door was opened the spring was extended precariously close to Eli's cage. Eli was just able to twang the spring with his longest massive finger. No matter where I worked in the health center I could hear the monotonous twang as he plucked at it with regularity.

In the back of my mind, I knew that someday he would grasp the spring with his whole hand. I did not think that I would actually see it happen, but I did. Eli was in late adolescence and was growing rapidly toward adulthood.

I was heading back to the orangutans' area after checking on the other animals under my care at the center. When I rounded the corner, I stopped in amazement. Eli had a full grasp of the spring and was pulling it into his cage. He resembled a giant hairy Robin Hood pulling a long bow to its limit. The whole garage door assembly bent towards the cage, and then he grabbed that. He pulled with all his might and ended up pulling bolts through a cracking and splintering four-by-four. By the time we were able to remove the assembly, he had tied the metal spring into several knots.

After I witnessed that incident, I added a foot or two onto the already respectful distance that I walked from his cage. And there were more incidents to follow.

Eli delighted in breaking things. One day he managed to stuff his whole body underneath his sleeping bench. The sleeping bench was welded securely to the bars of his cage about eighteen inches off the floor. Eli flexed every muscle in his powerful body. The two-inch by six-inch boards that were bolted to the sleeping bench cracked, then shattered all over the floor of his cage. Eli chose the largest board and fashioned it into a lever. He jammed the lever between the chain that secured the door and the bars of his cage. He pulled with all of his strength but succeeded only in breaking the lever. We were glad.

The most frightening incident occurred at feeding time at the health center. It was one o'clock in the afternoon and the vet and I were just finishing our lunch. A bloodcurdling, bone-chilling scream exploded the afternoon stillness and we looked at each other, both knowing what was happening. Ken, the keeper in the cage room, was in Eli's grasp. If we didn't get there quick Ken's chances of survival were slim to none. We leaped out of our chairs and headed for the cage room with reckless abandon. I veered off to grab the capture gun that always intimidated Eli. He wouldn't know if it were loaded or not. The doctor unlocked the cage room door and we burst through the opening together. Ken was screaming at the top of his lungs and we were hoping that we were not too late to save a hand or fingers. As we rounded the corner we saw that other help had arrived before us. Ken's senior keeper was poised to swing a shovel at Eli's hand. Ken had managed to turn his arm so that Eli could not pull it through the bars. Eli was trying his best to turn his arm while the senior keeper was trying to get a line on hitting Eli's hand with the shovel. The senior took a powerful swing. This was no time to hold back. Eli was mean but he wasn't stupid, and he removed his hand at the last possible second. The shovel connected with Ken's arm, causing him much more injury than Eli had.

Ken rolled backwards a safe distance from the cage, looked up at the senior keeper, smiled a relieved smile and said, "Whose side are you on anyway?"

Eli wouldn't let you like him. Because of his meanness I gave him satisfactory, but not exceptional, care. There were many times that Sally procured treats that I denied Eli. I didn't mind cleaning up after Sally when I had given her a magazine to look at, but I did Eli. The bottom line was Sally was easy to love but Eli wasn't. I really had to force myself to be nice to him.

As time passed I learned the difference between the good keepers and the great. The great simply gave their best to all their animals whether their animals performed or not.

I'm sure that this is what God expects from Christians. Jesus shares a verse that haunts me when I try to apply it to my life. It may be found in Luke 6:27–36. See how it affects you.

What's It to You?

But I say to you that hear, love your enemies, do good to those who hate you, bless those who curse you, pray for those who abuse you. To him who strikes you on the cheek, offer the other also; and to him that takes away your coat do not withhold even your shirt. Give to everyone who begs from you; and of him who takes away your goods do not ask them again.

And as you wish that men would do to you, do so to them. If you love those who love you, what credit is that to you? For even sinners love those that love them. And if you do good to those who do good to you, what credit is that to you? For even sinners do the same. And if you lend to those from whom you hope to receive, what credit is that to you? Even sinners lend to sinners, to receive as much again. But love your enemies, and do good, and lend, expecting nothing in return; and your reward will be great, and you will be sons of the Most High; for He is kind to the ungrateful and the selfish. Be merciful even as your Father is merciful.

Think it over.

The Black Widow

The greatest lesson I have learned from the animals was not learned at the zoo. It was learned in a mossy, moldy greenhouse in the backyard of a lady I was sure was a witch.

Spring was just giving way to summer. School was almost out, and like all eight-year-old boys I was looking forward to three months of no shoes, except on Sunday, and a creative string of adventures yet to be lived out. My mother was just beginning to fix dinner when the afternoon stillness was broken by the persistent ring of the front doorbell. At the door stood an older man. His tie was loosened and he was drenched with perspiration. He wiped the sweat from his forehead and began his to-the-point presentation, one that he had probably given fifty times before coming to our front door.

"Hello Ma'am. My name is Edgar Beasly and I'm from the health department. We are going door-to-door to alert people to the fact that they need to spray for black widow spiders. I bet you have already noticed that there are more spiders than usual. Doctors are reporting many bites that they feel are probably black widow bites. Last week a little girl nearly died from one. So we're here to warn you that we are having an epidemic of black widow spiders in California. This sometimes happens after a real wet spring."

He handed my mother a little book and said, "Ma'am, here's a pamphlet that gives you some real important information about black widows. It shows you what they look like and more importantly what their webs look like. We'd sure be much obliged if you'd spray."

When Mr. Beasly left, my mother scanned the pamphlet. She stared at me with legitimate concern and said, "Gary, if I ever catch you so much as walking by a black widow spider web, I'll spank your back side shiny. Do you understand me, young man?"

I nodded that I did and she handed me the pamphlet. I was fascinated. On the cover was a menacing picture of a female black widow. She looked large and was posed so that she revealed the red hourglass on the underside of her shiny black abdomen. The pamphlet made note that she lived in an irregular web that would likely be found in dark places like garages, wood piles, and under cabinets.

The section that most caught my interest was entitled, "The Bite of the Black Widow Spider." It said that a person who was bitten might experience the following symptoms: discoloration at the site of the bite, nausea, a severe headache, unusual swelling, labored breathing, and blurred vision. It concluded that some children even died from the bite of the black widow spider.

My mother never realized that she had just provided a road map for my next great adventure, a black widow safari. I couldn't wait to tell my best friend, Doug, about the greatest idea of my life.

"Now here it is, Doug. On Saturday morning my parents will be gone for three hours. I figure that will give us time to catch ten black widow spiders. We can take those bandits down to Eliot Junior High School and dump them on this red ant hill that I found. It will be great. The red ants will come streaming out to protect their home and there will be a scary fight. The red ants will win and we will have done our part in Altadena's battle to fight the black widows."

"What if we get bit?" Doug asked.

"We're not going to let those child-killers get us. We'll be real careful. Hey, you're not going to chicken out on me, are you?"

"Well, no," Doug added defensively.

I made Doug perform the bloodbrother handshake and promise not to tell any living soul what we were going to do at 8:30 Saturday morning. He took the oath, knowing that if he broke it his teeth and hair would fall out. I found an old peanut butter jar and poked a few holes in its lid. We didn't want any of the spiders dying before they got a chance to fight the red ants. We chose a two-foot stick for catching the spiders, and then we hid our safari gear behind the garage until Saturday.

As soon as my parents left to go shopping, I ran to Doug's house. He was already waiting for me in his front yard. We grabbed our gear and headed for my backyard. I had already located several webs. On the way there we ran into another good friend, Eric, who was coming over to see if we could play. We finally decided that we'd better let him in, but we made him take an even more solemn oath than Doug had taken.

"What kind of oath?" asked Eric.

"The kind that if you break it something scary happens."

Eric really wanted in so he took the oath.

"I, Eric . . ."

The Black Widow

"I, Eric . . ."

". . . promise never to tell about the black widow safari."

". . . promise never to tell about the black widow safari."

"If I do the Devil will make my mother's hair fall out."

"What?"

"You heard me, Eric. Do you want in or not?"

"It's just that I don't want the Devil around my mom."

"Are you planning to tell someone?"

"No . . . ."

"Then you don't have anything to worry about. There's a reason for this, Eric. You're not very good at keeping secrets and this will help you."

"Okay," said Eric. "If I do the Devil will make my mother's hair fall out."

"That wasn't so bad, was it?" asked Doug.

We walked down our long overgrown driveway and ran right into my twelve-year-old brother, Steve. Before we could stop him, Eric blurted out, "Guess what, Steve? We're going to catch ten black widow spiders and dump them on a red ant hill. Isn't that neat?"

My brother then treated us to the words we least liked to hear. "YOU GUYS ARE TOO YOUNG!"

Boy, I hated those words. Steve told us we were too young to catch black widow spiders, but agreed it sounded like a great idea. He offered to catch the spiders for us, and if we were good he would let us hold the jar.

As we followed my brother to our backyard, I held up my fist to Eric and said, "I'm never going to tell you a secret again. I hope you're thinking about what you just did to your mother, you oathbreaker."

I sadly handed over the catching stick to my brother and Doug reluctantly handed the peanut butter jar to me. Eric was trying to visualize his mother bald and wondering if she would know that it was his fault.

It took only a minute to discover the first spider. She was residing behind our tool shed. Her web was spun between the fence and the shed and bore the evidence of many a successful hunt. The dried bodies of three moths and two flies were mute reminders of her deadly capacities.

We crowded behind Steve to watch him catch the first of the ten spiders. He managed to get her on the end of the stick and called for me to open the jar. With trembling hands I opened the jar, and with a tap of the stick it received its first prisoner. She was medium sized and looked none to happy about being caught. She looked just like the spider on the pamphlet, and when I lifted the jar we were able to see the bright red hourglass on her shiny black abdomen.

As the jar began to fill up, my job became more and more difficult. The fifth spider attached a web to the lid so that when I opened the jar for the sixth spider I pulled the fifth across my hand.

After we had caught eight spiders we faced a dilemma. We ran out of spiders to catch on our property. Steve wanted to stop at eight, but I insisted that since we had agreed to catch ten that's exactly the number we should catch. Steve gave in, but he had no idea as to where we should hunt next. Eric, who had been the quiet observer on the safari, made a great suggestion. "I bet the evil queen of the black widow spiders lives in Mrs. Brown's greenhouse." Mrs. Brown lived next door to Doug, and all the neighborhood children were really afraid of her. She hated small children and would call the police on them if they even set foot on her property. Some of us were convinced that she was a witch and could cast spells that could keep us under her power and things like that.

What made Eric's idea so attractive was that catching the spiders had become too easy, and besides, my brother Steve was having all the fun. It was such a great idea that Eric was forgiven for breaking the oath and we told him so.

He said he was glad because he couldn't get used to the idea of having a bald mother. He said he thought it might be embarrassing.

Doug suggested that we sneak onto Mrs. Brown's property from his backyard. Her greenhouse was in the very back of her backyard, so Doug's suggestion was taken. We peered over Doug's fence into the untrimmed jungle that made up her yard and concluded that she was not outside. One at a time we dropped into forbidden territory and slipped silently into the greenhouse.

It was damp and dark, musty and moldy—perfect for black widows. We all felt that Mrs. Brown would jump out and grab us at any minute, so we asked Eric to keep watch.

Underneath her gardening bench was a five-gallon red clay pot. It was the kind my mother used to pot a small palm tree. It was turned upside down and resting on three red bricks. Steve and Doug turned it over very slowly and carefully. We each drew in our breath at what we saw. At the bottom of that clay pot was the largest black widow we had ever seen. She was fat and seemed to be throbbing with poison. She was protecting her silky white egg sac, and unlike the other spiders, she was simply not afraid of the stick.

After considerable effort, Steve was able to get the deadly giant on the end of the stick. He called for me to open the jar. I shook the jar until I was able to count the eight spiders we had already captured. Carefully, I turned the lid and removed it from the jar. I stood there with trembling hands while Steve brought the stick to the mouth of the jar. Just at the moment he was going to tap she made a jump for it. She landed right between my bare feet. I backed away, and in the excitement I forgot to put the lid back on the jar. My full attention was directed to the escapee between my feet, and I watched with rapt attention as my brother struggled to get her on the stick.

I failed to notice that a medium sized female was crawling out of the jar and onto the back of my hand. Slowly, I became aware of an eerie sensation and stared in disbelief at the little killer that was taking a morning stroll on my hand. I let the jar slip through my fingers, and black widows began to run everywhere. They mattered little anymore. The game was over. I was unable to speak words that had meaning but I managed a pretty good sound. I believe that phonetically it sounded a little like "yaaaaaaAAAAAAAAAAA!" My brother looked at me and it was clear that he was experiencing fear also.

Now I believe that our fear was of different natures. The fear that I was experiencing was because for the first time in my life I really believed that I was going to die. Not like in Cowboys and Indians where you could get up again, but the sort of death where everything goes dark, and after that I wasn't sure what would happen. It took all my strength to keep from fainting. I could feel every foot-fall of the spider on the back of my hand. I stayed perfectly still.

I begged my brother with my tear-filled eyes to please get the spider off my hand. He moved his index finger in a flicking position to within an inch of the spider. I held my breath and wanted to close my eyes, but I was afraid that if I did it would be for the last time. The spider stopped as if to consider what threat the finger was going to pose, and when she did, Steve flicked with all his might. The spider went flying. I have never felt a greater sense of relief in my life. Neither have I before or since learned a more important truth. Someday I am going to die.

How you feel about that truth has everything to do with how you prepare for it. If you have no belief in God or a future existence, then it really doesn't matter how you live your life. On the other hand, if you do believe in God, then everything you do matters. The Bible has two verses that really intrigue me:

> . . . it is appointed for men to die once and after this comes judgment . . . .
>
> Hebrews 9:27

We were designed to die. To die once is part of what being a man is all about. We have an appointment with death and nothing we can do will make us early or late. Listen to what James has to say concerning his view of life and death.

> Come now, you who say, "Today or tomorrow, we shall go to such and such a city, and spend a year there and engage in business and make a profit." Yet you do not know what your life will be like tomorrow. You are just a vapor that appears for a little while and vanishes away. Instead you ought to say, "If the Lord wills we shall live and do this or that."
>
> James 4:13–15

The Scripture clearly teaches that there is a God, and what we do matters a great deal to Him. It is also clear that whatever it is that we're going to accomplish needs to be accomplished before we die. The wisest man who ever lived wrote a dissertation on his search for truth and wisdom. His final words and conclusions are as follows:

> The end of the matter; all has been heard. Fear God and keep His commandments; for this is the whole duty of man. For God will bring every deed into judgment, with every secret thing, whether good or evil.
>
> Ecclesiastes 12:13–14

Protect Us from Those Who Protect Us

Cowboys and Indians, cats and dogs, Russians and Americans, security guards and animal keepers—they are all classical enemies. I'll bet you are surprised about security guards and animal keepers. I suppose this statement needs an explanation.

Security guards and animal keepers have a built-in basis for misunderstanding. It begins with the way they dress. Security guards wear neatly pressed uniforms, ties, and their shoes are so shiny that you may catch a glimpse of your own reflection as they pass by. Their fingernails look manicured and their hands are soft and smooth; no callouses need apply, thank you. By quitting time they are still neatly pressed and should they walk by, you may pick up the delicate remembrance of their shaving lotion as it echoes their departure. What can I say? They are eight-by-ten glossies.

Animal keepers dress in work clothes, dark brown pants and tan shirts. They perform hard physical labor and they sweat profusely. By morning break they may smell like twenty minutes of brisk basketball. Their shoes never shine and shouldn't even be discussed in mixed company. Their hands are weathered and calloused and could be used to plane a door. They are of the earth.

Security deals with the public. They know little of the animals and they are proud of it. They couldn't tell you the difference between a wallaby and a wombat.

Keepers talk animals, breathe animals, and dream animals. Do you want to know where animal keepers go on their vacations? To other zoos. That should tell you something.

The fact that security knows little about animals is not the rub. No indeed. The real problem is that keepers never see security guards do anything that remotely resembles work. They see them walk by, but zoo patrons do that. They see them drive by, and that's even worse because that's accomplished in a sitting position. As far as the keepers can observe, security just walks back and forth, drives back and forth, takes coffee breaks, and gets paid for it.

In all fairness, we had a fine security staff at the zoo, and still do. But there were some guards who seemed to reinforce all the suspicions and accusations that the keepers made about them. Let me illustrate.

In 1969 our Australian dingo dogs had puppies—five yellow balls of mischief that charmed every passerby. The keeper that cared for them played with them every chance he got, and they became very tame. They knew no strangers and spent a good deal of their day at the front of their cage licking people's fingers and accepting as much affection as they could solicit. Now if you know wild animals, a dingo dog is a very distinctive breed. But if you don't, it's just another old yeller dog. It looks like a cross between a German shepherd and a yellow Labrador retriever. You might find something similar any day you visited your local animal shelter.

The zoo was a popular hangout for hippies in the late sixties. One of them formed an affection with the dingo pups and conceived a plan. It was a simple plan. Smuggle wire cutters under your trench coat and cut just enough wire so that you might liberate one puppy. If you came on a weekday, no one would ever notice what you had done. That's just what he did. He and his girlfriend paid their admission and walked straight to our Australian section. I'm confident that she stood watch while he labored to snip the wire in six places. He bent up the wire and—presto!—he possessed his own dingo pup.

Oh, but he wasn't out of the woods yet. He was two-fifths of a mile from the front gate. He had picked the most wiggly puppy of the five. It was noisy, too. They began to walk to the front gate when they were stopped. Can't you imagine how their hearts began to pound?

The security guard spoke with practiced authority, "Hey! What you got under that coat? You want to show it to me?" The hippie looked paralyzed. He opened up his coat and extended the wiggly puppy toward the security guard who patted it on the head and said, "I didn't want to hold your puppy, I just wanted to see it. Didn't you folks see the 'No Pets' sign at the front gate? We don't allow pets because they might give our animals a new disease or something. I'm afraid that I'm going to have to escort you to the front gate and make sure that you get the pup off the premises."

That's just what that security guard did. He gave them the equivalent of a police escort right to the front gate while the hippie and his girlfriend apologized all the way to their car. They apologized so much that the security guard began to apologize for the size of the small "no pets allowed" sign.

Boy, did the keepers have fun with that story. They said that it was a good thing the hippie didn't try to steal an elephant or the security guard might have gotten a hernia helping him carry it out.

Not too long after that, a night security guard offered the *coup de grâce* to any hopes of a reconciliation. A gentle female chimpanzee escaped from her cage at the old zoo two miles away, where the chimps were being held until their quarters at the health center became available once again. It was three in the morning, and the security guard caught a glimpse of the ambling ape in the high beams of his security vehicle. He radioed the security center at the main zoo for instructions as to what he should do. The security center phoned Dr. Sedgwick at home and advised him of the emergency. They asked him what the guard should do. Not knowing that it was one of the very gentle females, Dr. Sedgwick advised the security officer on the scene to do anything necessary to keep the chimp from leaving the area. It could be a very dangerous animal roaming the neighborhoods surrounding Griffith Park. As Dr. Sedgwick was hanging up the phone, he thought that it may have been better if he had not made the chimp seem so dangerous. He recalled that the particular security guard on the scene was a gun enthusiast. Dr. Sedgwick arrived at the old zoo ten minutes too late. The sweet young female was already dead. She had been shot to death by the night security guard.

The officer's story was that he had stepped out of his vehicle to follow the chimp and she charged him. The examination revealed that the chimp had been shot in the back. Although Dr. Sedgwick tried his best to explain that he had set the security guard up to be terrified, the keepers just wouldn't buy it. They hounded that man until the day he quit the zoo!

I have many times since tried to put myself in the place of that security guard. The zoo is an eerie place at night and surpasses a graveyard for downright frightfulness. I don't believe in ghosts, but I do believe in animals. The years have proven that animals do get out, and you could never be sure that you were not sharing a path with an escaped lion or a bear. The security guard couldn't have known which chimps were dangerous and which ones were not. Nobody could have known in the dark. I'm not sure what I would have done if a chimp approached me on a dark night at the old zoo. Well, it was a long while before the hard feelings were abated.

About the time they had, something else happened. It was five-thirty in the evening on a Thursday and the red phone began to ring at the security office. It was an ominous signal. It meant that one of the keepers at the reptile house had been bitten by a deadly snake. The system is arranged so that as soon as the keeper is bitten, he could walk to a red phone and simply take it off the hook. This would cause the red phone to ring in the security office and trigger a whole sequence of events to unfold. Supervisors would be notified, County General would be called, and a security guard would rush to the reptile house to assist with emergency transportation.

Everything went like clockwork except for the part where the security guard rushes to the reptile house to provide transportation. He rushed to the reptile house, all right, and he rang the doorbell. Nobody answered, so he rang it again and again. It wouldn't be difficult to deduce that the man inside was probably unconscious by now and couldn't answer the door. So thought the security guard. He walked around the outside of the building yelling, "Is anybody hurt in there?" And of course he received no reply. One of the senior animal keepers leaving a bit late for home overheard the yelling and ran to investigate.

"What's wrong?" asked the out-of-breath senior keeper.

"The red phone's been pulled. It's ringing like crazy down at the security center."

"What are you doing out here then, you dumb

———————?" he yelled. The senior keeper rushed inside the building and searched the maze of interconnected rooms that made up the reptile house. Nobody was there. It was later discovered that a water pipe had burst and shorted out the red phone line.

When the senior keeper came out of the building he was blazing mad. "What's your problem, son?" he asked.

"I'm afraid of snakes, okay?" replied the embarrassed guard.

"Son, this is a heck of a time to admit it. A man could have lost his life because of you, you know."

The question was posed after that incident, "If security's job is to protect us from the people, who's going to protect us from security?"

Even so, my mind was to be changed forever as to security's worth. I'm deathly allergic to the sting of honeybees, and one sparkling morning I was stung on the arm. I staggered to the chief keeper's office and announced my dilemma. He was familiar with the gravity of my situation and notified security. With all that had gone on before, I had reservations about putting my life in security's hands. I was amazed when they arrived at the chief's office in less than forty-five seconds, and in no time we were speeding along the freeway to a hospital in nearby Glendale. From the sting to the treatment, less than eight minutes had passed. They were kind to me, and after the incident I was asked several times how I was doing by the security guards who had helped me out. I felt just like the man who had been robbed in the Good Samaritan story. It changed my whole perspective of the security guards when they helped me in that crisis.

As I began to talk with the security staff, I found out they were really a super group of guys. Their job was with people and mine was with animals. I can tell you right now I wouldn't have traded jobs with those guys if I were paid twice my salary.

Have you read the parable of the Good Samaritan lately? You can find it in Luke 10:25–37. Read it. Then ask yourself if you have been building up a prejudice. Chances are that the Lord is calling you to love the person who has come to mind.

I have found C. S. Lewis's *Mere Christianity* to be a most helpful book. It makes me think more than any other book that I have ever read. In the chapter entitled "Charity" resides a most provocative paragraph.

I pointed out in the chapter on Forgiveness that our love for ourselves does not mean that we like ourselves. It means that we wish our own good. In the same way Christian Love (or charity) for our neighbors is quite a different thing from liking or affection. We "like" or are "fond of" some people, and not of others. It is important to understand that this natural "liking" is neither a sin nor a virtue, anymore than your likes and dislikes of food are a sin or a virtue. It is just a fact. But of course, what we do about it is either sinful or virtuous.

What we should do when we find that we are not liking someone is to perform an act of kindness toward him. It is easier to love someone you are helping than someone you are hurting.

What If?

I have played the "What If?" game since childhood. You have too, I'll bet. The really great players are blessed or cursed with active imaginations. In a group of people, What If-ers are sure to be the ones who create the most enthusiasm or inspire the most fear.

I began developing my skills when I was very young, and by the fifth grade I was quite capable of What If-ing with the best of them. My friend, Doug, and I had even What If-ed our way into believing there was a bigfoot creature residing in a nearby canyon. Yes, sir, I am fully convinced that I was What If-Ing at high school level—maybe higher.

What If-ing carries with it an awesome power. It is the power of suggestion. The power does not diminish as one gets older. It increases.

By the time I had reached my twenty-fifth year of life

I had turned What If-ing into a science. If there were an Olympics for What If-ers I would have been in the decathalon. If there had been an Olympics of that type it would have been held at the Los Angeles Zoo. That's where the best What If-ers trained. If you would ever like to see them in training, visit the zoo at breaktime. They will What If like crazy for fifteen minutes out of every twenty minutes of breaktime.

I remember the day that a group of veteran keepers got together for what may be the finest single session of What If-ing in the history of man. It was the summer of 1968. It was really warm for ten o'clock in the morning and the air was crystal clear, which was odd for Los Angeles. The heat brought more keepers than usual who thought an ice-cold soft drink might just hit the spot. We gathered at the North American snack bar and filled the cement picnic tables that circled the building. We enjoyed the shade and the fraternity.

It didn't take long for the conversation to turn into a What If-ing session.

Don got us started. "Did you hear that some hermit has been sneaking into the zoo at night, crawling into exhibits and stealing food from the animals? Guy's nuts, I bet. What if a guy like that got hold of a set of keys? He could let a lot of animals out in a short amount of time."

Dale added, "What if a guy like that got into the reptile house? Can you imagine what Griffith Park would be like with cobras and mambas and all sorts of vipers? You couldn't get anybody to come to the zoo for years. There'd be a big lawsuit if anybody got bit. You could count on that."

"What if that guy let Bosco the cape buffalo out? Cape buffalos have knocked boxcars off train tracks in Africa. I'd hate to come into the zoo some morning and find Bosco looking at me. He charges the fence now. Can you imagine what fun he'd have really knocking people around like beach balls? Did you ever watch him stand behind his fence and go into a rage? He trembles and salivates, moans and groans, and then he charges. I swear someday he won't have to wait to be let out. He's going to knock his fence down or come through the side of the barn. That Bosco is something, all right."

John decided it was his moment and spoke. "Ivan's the one that gives me nightmares. What if some nutball let him out?" We all got real quiet because John had just verbalized everybody's nightmare. Ivan the polar bear was the most feared animal at the zoo. John seized the opportunity to run with the moment he had created.

"I was here the day Ivan killed Nanatchka. She was a pretty bear. Ivan went right after her. That's just what he'd do to us, you know." John paused again for effect. Everybody stayed silent as they nursed their own private fears of Ivan. John resumed his manipulation. "Bears don't kill you right off."

All the keepers but one left breaktime glad that they didn't have to care for Ivan. Ivan's keeper was a little slow leaving the picnic tables, and he thought about Ivan all the way back to the elephant seal pool. That "he" was me. What made John's What If more effective was the fact that only days before, one of the Kodiak bears had lifted his guillotine door and let all the other Kodiak bears out on exhibit just seconds after the keeper had finished cleaning. He'd be dead for sure if that bear had made his move any sooner. I wondered if Ivan could ever figure out how to open the door and let himself out.

Jim was a relief keeper, and on the way back from break I had discovered that he had been assigned to help me with my string. I had been busy acid-washing the elephant seal pool and was sadly behind. Ivan's exhibit had not been cleaned and neither were the penguins and pelicans on exhibit.

"Al Franklin asked me to clean Ivan's exhibit for you. He said you were behind because of acid-washing. I know the routine, so you don't have to show me anything."

"Thanks, Jim. I owe you one."

"Don't mention it."

Jim headed for the polar bear moat and I went to the pelagic bird exhibit. I remembered that Jim had looked very impressed by John's dissertation and it gave me an idea. Keepers are incurable practical jokers, and they specialize in scare jokes. I knew the cleaning routine for the polar bear moat backwards and forwards. I had performed it hundreds of times myself. Jim would just now be opening up the back door to the moat. He would prop that door open to ventilate the area and walk forward five steps to unlock a sliding door. He would pull it open and slide it shut again. He would turn and look at Ivan who was already looking at him. He would be impressed by the size of Ivan's massive paws. Ivan weighed nine hundred and fifty pounds. He stood nearly ten feet tall. He was 100 percent nightmare and never missed a chance to swipe at a keeper. Ivan was above all things a killer. Jim would lock the guillotine door handle into place so that no one could let Ivan out on him. Then he would open three more chain-link doors that would give him access to the outdoor exhibit. Ivan's pool was already drained, so Jim would grab the one-inch hose, put on the high-pressure nozzle, and turn on the water. The surge of pressure would jar his arm and the noise inside the grotto would be deafening. He would then drag the hose down the dimly lit hallway. He would pull it out into the morning sun and begin cleaning the exhibit.

I timed it so that I was silently entering the back door just as Jim was beginning to clean. I stopped at the hose bib long enough to turn the hose on and off. It makes the guy outside think his hose is kinked and he will give it a dynamic tug to relieve the problem. After doing that a couple of times, I proceeded to stalk my prey down the dimly lit hallway. All I had to do was to follow the hose. As I crept up behind him I could see that he was completely involved with his task. This was going to be too easy. I stepped to within reach of my prey and let out a mighty roar. Now polar bears don't roar, but even the finest keeper would have forgotten that fact under the circumstances. I simultaneously grabbed his shoulder and side. I had never seen anybody try to climb a high-pressure hose before. But that day I did. I'll have to give Jim credit for one thing, he never let go of the hose through all the animation that he achieved. Boy, was he angry. People sometimes get that way when you get them to abandon their dignity. Jim was a soft-spoken man, but he said some words that I had never heard before or since.

Jim had been set up by the negative power of suggestion. What If-ing had taken its toll. Because we are fallen creatures we are prone to think negatively. Our What If-ing mechanisms turned inward usually create apprehension and fear. We become victims of our own thinking patterns. If we allow that to happen, we become cowards, too afraid to make a move, any move, for fear we might fail. Our imagination has the potential to extend our faith or destroy it.

What If-ing prevented two million Israelites from entering the Promised Land. Joshua and Caleb believed God, but everyone else forgot that the Lord would fight for them. Their imaginations took over.

Moses described the effect of the What If-ers in Deuteronomy 1:28–33.

> "Whither are we going up? Our brethren have made our hearts melt, saying, 'The people are greater and taller than we; the cities are great and fortified up to heaven; and moreover we have seen the sons of the Anakim there.' Then I said to you, 'Do not be in dread or afraid of them. The LORD your God who goes before you will himself fight for you, just as he did for you in Egypt before your eyes, and in the wilderness, where you have seen how the LORD your God bore you, as a man bears his son, in all the way that you went

until you came to this place.' Yet in spite of this word you did not believe the LORD your God, who went before you in the way to seek you out a place to pitch your tents, in fire by night, to show you by what way you should go, and in the cloud by day."

Gideon hesitated before his heroic acts by speculating that God might have left him. He was asking "What if God decides not to stay by my side?"

We have heard it said, "A coward dies a thousand deaths, a brave man just one."

Romans 12 tells us that we should "renew our minds that we may prove what is the will of God." We must change our way of thinking so that it conforms to God's will.

Negative: What if I share my faith in Christ with that person and they think I'm a fruitcake or a religious nut?

Positive: What if I share my faith with that person? Maybe they will come to know Him and find peace, joy, and salvation.

Negative: What if I said no? Maybe he'd think I was a prude. Maybe he wouldn't ask me out anymore.

Positive: What if I said no? I'd keep my self-respect. And if he doesn't ask me out again, God will provide better.

What If-ing is in its negative context nothing more than worry. And we are commanded not to worry.

Have no anxiety about anything, but in everything by prayer and supplication with thanksgiving let your requests be made known to God. And the peace of God, which passes understanding, will keep your hearts and minds in Christ Jesus.

Philippians 4:6–7

How do we change if we are worriers (and I am)? It's a matter of forcing ourselves into new ways of thinking. Philippians 4:8 gives us the formula.

Finally, brethren, whatever is true, whatever is honorable, whatever is just, whatever is pure, whatever is lovely, whatever is gracious, if there is any excellence, if there is anything worthy of praise, **think about these things.**

"But Lord, what if I can't?"
"No excuses, My child! I will be with you."

The Intervention

I couldn't say I hadn't been warned. I had been . . . and by the most respected keeper at the zoo. He had walked right up to me two months before and said, "Richmond, anybody tell you about the kudu?" (A kudu is an extremely large, six-hundred-pound antelope with horns that spiral thirty-six inches above its head. It is tan and white with soft vertical stripes on its muscular sides. The females are more delicate and have no horns.)

"No, Jack," I responded. "Is there something I should know?"

"Be careful," he said matter of factly. Then he walked back to his section.

No one knew more about African hoofstock than Jack Badal. He had been given the Marlin Perkins Award for his amazing accomplishments with hoofstock. So if he said I should be careful, then careful I would be.

I did a little research and discovered that the male kudu becomes sexually mature at two years. Our male had just reached that milestone. Smaller sixty-pound antelopes can become a bit dangerous during breeding season, but a six-hundred-pound greater kudu could be lethal. Even lions avoided such an animal.

I began to watch and noticed some very subtle changes. First, the kudu began to withdraw from human contact. Then he took to sharpening his horns on the granite walls of his compound. I watched him carefully, knowing of his potential.

When I worked this section I would arrive at the zoo at 4:45 A.M. and check my animals. If anything happened during the night, I wanted to be the one who discovered it. If everything checked out, I would spend the next hour reading at the golf course clubhouse adjacent to the zoo, then begin my 6:00 A.M. to 2:30 P.M. schedule.

I'll never forget a June morning in 1968. It was an hour before sunrise and very foggy. The zoo is eerie when it's dark and downright scary when the fog is draping the streetlights and muffling the sounds. I walked by the impala and noticed that they were standing with their ears cocked toward the kudu barn. Henry, the saddle-bill stork, was pacing. Normally he would be on one leg asleep. Something was up! I hurried my pace.

When I reached the kudus, my heart was gripped with terror. The male was viciously attacking the females. Unless I was successful in separating them, the females would be killed. I knew what was happening. In the wild the females would be giving off a scent which attracts and provokes the males. The males would fight each other for days; and when the strongest emerged, they would claim the females and mating would begin. In a zoo there are no extra males to fight and the females are not ready to mate. The male becomes enraged when the females reject him and they become the recipients of his wrath.

The Intervention

They were in their night quarters, a small forty-by-forty-foot corral adjacent to where they were put on public display during the day. It was the largest yard in the zoo. I thought the females might live if I was successful in letting them out so they could avoid him. The problem was that in order to let them out, I had to enter and walk completely across the small corral. The male didn't look as if he wanted company, but something had to be done now. I grabbed a rake and shovel and placed them in a wheelbarrow. I unlocked the gate and stepped into the corral. Everything became still . . . and it seemed as if I had entered a bad dream. The male stared at me and shook his head in challenge. I whistled "Amazing Grace" and began to back across the corral. He stalked me like a cat stalks a mouse. His eyes were full of rage. I finally reached the other side and fumbled for the lock. I turned the key, keeping one eye on the enraged male who was standing fifteen feet in front of me. It clicked and I slid it out of the hasp. The male charged. I could see the finely sharpened tips of his horns headed for my chest. I threw myself against the gate. It gave way and I fell backwards. There was a brown blur, a sickening thud, and a mournful cry. A female had run for the gate and taken my blow. I scrambled up the chain-link gate and cast myself out of the exhibit. I landed on my back seven feet below on a thick bed of ivy where, for several seconds, I pondered the question "Am I alive?" My heart was pounding and I was soaking wet. I took those to be good signs.

After thirty minutes of intense efforts, I was able to separate the male from the females. He was locked in a barn for two weeks and let out when the females were ready for him. Both females gave birth several months later. One of them always wore a scar where the male gored her as he attempted to kill me. Her saving my life had not been intentional, but I always gave her special treatment after that. I loved her for it.

It occurred to me that this was not the first time some-one had taken punishment for me. It had happened before, only on that occasion my Savior had known exactly what He was doing and what it would mean.

But He was pierced through for our transgressions, He was crushed for our iniquities; the chastening for our well-being fell upon Him, and by his scourging we are healed.

Isaiah 53:5

Have you thanked Jesus lately? Perhaps it's time you did.

Counting the Cost

When I was young my father told me to always count the cost. It was good but wasted advice. I didn't know how. I had too little experience with life and too much pride to ask anyone who had seen the price tags. Looking back, I'm fairly sure that if someone had given me their cost estimate, I would have thought I could get it for less.

I think this flaw is inherent in humanity, especially the young, and is also the reason why the German philosopher Hegel wrote, "The only thing we've learned from history is that we have learned nothing from history."

I remember the oral interviews I took to become an animal keeper. I was twenty-three years old. A salty old veteran of hundreds, maybe thousands, of interviews looked at me over his rimless glasses and asked, "You've told us what you think will be the fun parts of working at the zoo. What do you think will be some of the difficulties or unpleasantries?"

Never having worked at a zoo, I didn't have a clue. I had so romanticized zoo work that I couldn't think of anything bad. I had to say something, so I blurted out, "I guess I'll go home with my clothes smelling bad sometimes."

He looked at me meditatively. His expression said, "If you want to say more you can." But I couldn't think of anything more, so he broke the awkward silence and the interview continued.

I worked at the zoo for seven years, and all the good things that I had anticipated were a part of the package. But there were also costs . . . some very high costs. Let me share a few.

There were assaults on my dignity. The first animal to attack me was a small, very huffy male penguin that resented being chased out of a bunker onto exhibit. I was nearly kicked to death by an ostrich that was insulted when I failed to respond to his romantic advances. I was assigned to give a tetanus shot to a wild donkey that had stepped on a rusty nail. When I administered the shot to his flank, he returned the favor by kicking me so hard that I almost went through the barn door. I can still feel his "shot" on rainy days.

I was inches from being gored to death by a kudu, a large African antelope. He had mistaken me for a rival suitor. Later this same seven-hundred-pound herd bull did plunge his thirty-six-inch horns through another keeper's body. I was nipped by a rabid raccoon and had to go through the painful series of shots in the stomach. They were worse than I had imagined. I nearly died from the treatment (3 percent of the patients who undergo the Pasteur treatment die from it). I was consistently exposed to zoonosis, diseases transmissible from animals to man, many of which could prove to be fatal.

When I spoke out on behalf of the animals because of poor conditions, I was sent to the zoo's version of Siberia.

The section to which I was assigned had more work than a man could do well in eight hours, and most men who were sent there had quit with broken spirits. I discovered that I was allergic to dust and hay, and this section had more of both than any other section in the zoo. I developed chronic bronchitis and drifted into pneumonia on several occasions.

Oh, yes—and there were days when my clothes did smell bad, even terrible.

This is a very partial list, but I think you get the idea. I know something now for sure that was theoretical twenty years ago when I was hoping to work at the zoo. Anything really valuable has a price tag. M. Scott Peck's opening words in *The Road Less Traveled* are so very true.

> Life is difficult. This is a great truth, one of the greatest truths. It is a great truth because once we truly see this truth, we transcend it. Once we truly know that life is difficult—once we truly understand and accept it—then life is no longer difficult. Because once it is accepted, the fact that life is difficult no longer matters.

Life at its best will cost us something, and life lived at its best is lived for Jesus Christ. Jesus knows the price tag because He paid the price. Let's remember what He said:

> . . . If anyone wishes to come after Me, let him deny himself, and take up his cross, and follow Me. For whoever wishes to save his life shall lose it; and whoever loses his life for My sake and the gospel's shall save it. For what does it profit a man to gain the whole world and forfeit his soul?
>
> Mark 8:34–37

Paul spoke plainly when he wrote to the Philippians:

> For to you it has been granted for Christ's sake, not only to believe in Him, but also to suffer for His sake.
>
> Philippians 1:29

So as I read it, the cost is dying to ourselves and believing and being willing to suffer. Well, it's the least we can do for Him. He's done it for us. And we didn't even deserve it.

Think about these questions: What is my faith costing me? How am I demonstrating the value of my Lord, my family, and my church to the world around me? And why did the Lord think I was worth the price He paid for me?

As my father said, "You should always count the cost." I know what you mean now, Dad. I really do.

Badal

There are some men who are larger than life. Jack Badal is such a man.

I remember my first day as a new keeper at the Los Angeles Zoo. I was introduced to the chief keeper who in turn introduced me to one of his principal keepers. The principal keeper was responsible for one-half of the zoo's animal care and would that day introduce me to my senior keeper. Seniors are in charge of a section of exhibits, and keepers are in charge of what we call a "string."

The principal took a moment to size me up and began his introductory speech. "Richmond, there's a right way, a wrong way, and Jack Badal's way to do everything. But only Jack can do it his way, so you just work on getting it right."

Sensing that he had just shared something important, I seized the opportunity to insert a question. "Who is Jack Badal?"

"Jack works African hoofstock just up the road. If you see a man that wears a green baseball cap backwards, whistles while he works, and looks like he could have eaten a Sherman tank for breakfast, that is Jack Badal. He is real particular about who he talks to, and if he doesn't like you he won't talk to you at all. He knows more than anyone here and works harder too."

"He sounds like an interesting guy. I'll be looking forward to meeting him," I said with enthusiasm.

"Amazing is a better word I think," added the principal. "And by the way, don't bother asking him any questions about the animals. He won't answer them anyway."

"Why not?"

"Jack is from a different era. He's from the old school, the school of trade secrets. In the old days the keepers were divided into two groups; zookeepers and animal men. The zookeepers basically cleaned and fed wild animals. The animal men turned zookeeping into an art. The animal men knew what their animals were thinking, what they were feeling. They knew what to do to keep them from fighting and from becoming diseased. They knew how to encourage breeding. But they wouldn't pass their knowledge on because their knowledge was their job security. It was valuable, not to be given away just because someone asked for it. Their knowledge had been obtained through careful observation over a long period of time. So why should they give it away?"

I was assigned to the Eurasian section on the opposite side of the zoo from the African hoofstock. I didn't see Jack Badal for three weeks but I heard about him often. When people spoke about Jack, it was usually with awe bordering on reverence. All of the veteran keepers from the old Griffith Park Zoo had Badal stories. I remember hearing that he had single-handedly moved an adult ostrich into a crate for shipment after four men had failed in their joint attempt. I heard that Jack leaped off of a seven-foot wall and subdued a young buffalo so that the zoo vet could give it antibiotics.

One of the favorite stories that circulated for all seven years of my career concerned a strong disagreement. Jack had had it with another keeper who had lied about him, causing him to be accused of something he hadn't done. When Jack confronted him, the man was flippant and smart-mouthed. It apparently angered Jack so that he clenched his fists and considered taking a poke at the sarcastic troublemaker. The man knew he had stepped over a foolish line and looked terrified as Jack stood there shaking with anger. Jack had reached a point that required the release of inner tensions, so he hit the wall right next to the man's head. They say his fist passed through the wall into the next room. Jack stared into the shaken man's eyes for a moment and then left the room.

I'm not sure whether the stories were true or false. Perhaps they were half true. What was true was that Jack was a legend, and people are always adding to legends. Everyone agreed that Jack was our zoo's only animal man, maybe even the last animal man around.

Two years into my career I was assigned to be Jack's relief keeper, which meant that I would take care of Jack's string on his days off. I found my heart beating rapidly when my new senior keeper introduced me to Jack as his new relief man. When the senior keeper left, Jack broke the ice by asking, "Do you like African hoofstock?"

"I'm not sure, I've never worked them before. I want to learn everything I can while I'm at the zoo. It will be great working with you. I hear you're the best. Most of the guys think you're a legend."

Jack smiled and said, "Well you know what they say, 'A legend's feet are made of sand.'"

I knew right away that I was going to enjoy working with Jack. The man turned out to be twice as good as the legend.

"Follow me," he said as he led me to the sable antelope barn. Before we entered the barn he paused quietly at the fence and studied every one of the perfect specimens. His eyes searched quickly for anything that would tip him off to a need or problem. His animals were thriving. Their coats shone in the morning sun and they held their heads proudly. Their eyes had a special sparkle and their muscles rippled with energy. These antelope were neither too fat nor too thin, and their condition was the result of perfect care.

"These sable are really something," he said with quiet admiration. "The males have been known to kill lions. See this fence?" He pointed to the gate. It was bowed out as if it had been hit by a car. "That's where the bull hit the other day trying to get to a passerby. We don't go in with these guys."

I was glad. Jack looked at me to make sure that I was listening. I nodded that I had understood not to go in with these majestic creations with the deadly horns.

I had heard that Jack's barns were so immaculate you could eat your lunch off the floors. I'm sure the statement was true, but I never found the will to test it. He opened the door for my first look and I stepped inside. My eyes searched every corner, especially the stalls. After what he said about the sable antelope I wanted to be sure that we wouldn't be entering any area that was already occupied. All the animals were outside the barn on exhibit. My inspection ended with eye to eye contact with Jack. He had been watching me.

"You have the eyes of an animal man," he said.

"Why do you say that?" I asked.

"When we came into the barn you looked into every corner to see what was happening. That's what an animal man does. An animal man doesn't miss a thing. He checks everything out. You're going to be good if you stick with this business."

I counted that as the greatest compliment that I had

received at the zoo. Coming from Jack those were most encouraging words.

Jack trained me for two days and I can honestly say that I learned more that had practical value in those sixteen hours than I had learned in the previous two years at the zoo. Jack had turned little things into an art. Raking, for instance, became a subject for learning. He showed me how to position the angle of the rake for greater efficiency. I was able to cut my raking time in half. He showed me a technique for tossing dirt back through the rake tines while retaining the leaves and waste material. He showed me how to sculpture the yard to improve rain drainage. He packed the dirt down firmly and kept it from being dusty with frequent waterings. The end result was animals with clear lungs and hooves that seemed to wear down at just the perfect rate. I can't recall our ever needing to trim the hooves of any of the animals on Jack's string. Jack taught me to whistle while I worked. I felt like a dwarf now and then, but my animals never needed to watch for me if they could hear where in the exhibit I was. This practice really did relieve tension. Jack showed me a way to moisten the hay so that it was more enjoyable for the animals. He also showed me how to place the hay in different locations so that competition for the food was reduced. I found Jack to be colorful, knowledgeable, a great storyteller, efficient, the hardest worker I have ever met, and a dedicated Christian.

I asked Jack to explain his philosophy of animal keeping. His answers were thought provoking. He said, "Gary, I try to spend each day at the zoo so that I never regret yesterday. These animals provide a job for me. The pay I get feeds my family. I figure I owe them the best I can give. It's my job to take all the bad things out of their world and replace them with good things. They depend on me and I don't want to let them down."

Proverbs 12:10 always comes to my mind when I think of Jack. "A righteous man has regard for the life of his beast."

Jack was a living proverb. I did and still do consider Jack Badal the best in the business—the last of the great animal men.

Jack's skills were not limited to animal care. He was also one of the greatest animal trainers in history. He trained elephants for the zoo, and was especially fond of a lowland gorilla named Ramar. That gorilla performed tricks gorillas had never been taught before. Jack loved that animal, and his eyes sparkled whenever I asked him about Ramar. The day that Ramar became too large to be safely controlled came all too soon. I know that it broke Jack's heart to give him up to an eastern zoo, but it had to be done.

One of my favorite stories is one that Jack told me about how he became the trainer for the Los Angeles Zoo. They needed someone to train the elephants to walk the two miles to the new zoo. Three men applied.

Gary, they brought the three of us candidates into a waiting room and told us to please sit down. Animal trainers are a funny breed, and we didn't talk much while we were waiting for our turn to be interviewed. They called the first guy in and about two minutes later we heard a macaw squawking his head off. In another two minutes the first guy comes out. He's red-faced and doesn't say a word. He just leaves in a huff. The second guy goes in and the same thing happens again, only the bird is even louder than before. Number two comes out shaking his head, looks at me, rolls his eyes, and leaves. I wondered what was going on.

"Mr. Badal, would you please come in?" asked one of the interviewers. I said, "Yes, sir," and walked right into the room. There were some important men from city hall, and the zoo directors, of course. Right in the middle of the room was a large cage with a very nervous scarlet macaw. He was looking at everybody and rocking back and forth because he was still upset.

The director said, "So you want to be our trainer, Mr. Badal?"

Badal

"Yes, sir," I answered.

"We would like to get a little idea of your skills, Mr. Badal." They handed me a small bird net with about a two-foot handle and asked me if I would please take the macaw out of the cage for them.

I knew just what had been happening. The two guys ahead of me were manhandling the bird. They had most likely netted the bird, drug him out of the cage, and put him back in. That's why the bird was so upset. I hid the net behind my back and spoke quietly to the bird until I could see that he was calming down. Then I slowly and carefully opened the door and let him get used to that. I turned the net around and offered the handle to the bird. He stepped right on and I lifted him out of the cage slowly and stood before the interview board.

I said, "Now what would you like me to do with the bird?"

"Put him back in the cage, Mr. Badal. And congratulations—you are our new trainer."

In Jack's world he is the standard of excellence, admired by his peers and respected by his friends. He is the kind of person about whom it is said, "They don't make them like that anymore." As great as all of his accomplishments in the animal world are, they are excelled by the quality of his walk with Jesus Christ. You see, Jack lives his life according to Colossians 3:17:

And whatever you do, in word or deed, do everything in the name of the Lord Jesus, giving thanks to God the Father through him.

You Might
Have to Ask

Nothing is more frustrating than living with an unsolved mystery. That's how the zoo staff felt when every day at ten o'clock an old man would visit the children's zoo. He was tall and dignified, and his suit, vest, tie, overcoat, and shoes showed signs of considerable age and wear. With a cane in one hand and shopping bag in the other, he would walk to isolated spots and then look over his shoulder to see if anyone was watching. This, of course, aroused suspicion and the zoo staff began to watch him carefully. The following is what they observed.

He would open his shopping bag and reach in for slices of dry bread, which he scattered about the bench where he was seated. He then adjusted his pant legs and started pulling what seemed to be threads or something out from under his cuff. Wild ground squirrels would gather to eat the bread, and when they did he would leap up from the bench and raise his arms high in the air. On some occasions he would pound his lower legs and then retire to the men's room. At other times he would readjust his pant legs and begin to pull at the threads again. By noon, he was gone.

The old man was driving the staff crazy. And his behavior became the object of much conversation and theory, none of which was kind. He was labeled the "kook," the "pervert," and was thought to be strange. Some even wondered if he was safe around children.

His activities were brought to the attention of our director. Being a man unable to live with mystery, he watched the man through binoculars for several minutes, but was unable to determine what he was doing. He decided to take a direct approach, so he confronted the old gentleman personally.

"What are you doing, sir?" said the director. "You are driving the staff crazy." The old man, his head bowed, quietly explained. "I live on a fixed income, you see, and I can't afford much food. I'm squirrel fishing. I pass fishing line down my pant legs and put chunks of bread on treble hooks. When the squirrels reach for the bread . . . ."

The director raised his hand to stop the old gentleman from saying more. He could see the man looked humiliated. "To tell you the truth," said the director, "those squirrels are pests and you're probably helping us. It's just that if some child sees you . . . well, I think you understand." The director then took out his wallet and pressed ten dollars into the old man's wrinkled hand. "This is for hamburgers, okay?" The old man nodded gratefully, then left. We never saw him again.

It is so easy to think the worst, to make the wrong assumption. If people don't smile much or cease to talk to me, I rarely think to ask them why. I am ten times more likely to assign a wrong meaning to their silence. Often my last thought is that their silence may be the loudest cry for help that they are capable of making.

A VIEW FROM THE ZOO

The apostle Paul once wrote:

> Do nothing from selfishness or conceit, but with humility of mind let each of you regard one another as more important than himself; do not merely look out for your own personal interest, but also for the interests of others.
>
> Philippians 2:3–4

Is anybody in your life behaving strangely? Maybe it's time to ask what's going on.

Sins of the Fathers

When I was first transferred to the zoo health center I was introduced to the most heartless man I have ever known. It might surprise you, but the man was an animal keeper. He was responsible for the hillside string which included bison, tule elk, peccary, mule deer, axis deer, and a solitary mountain goat. Even though my main duties were in the health center, I became his relief keeper one day a week. I didn't mind hoofstock, in fact I loved them, but since he never did any work the area was always a mess by Friday. The first day we met he told me how proud he was that he was paid so much for so little work. He claimed that he never worked more than one hour a day.

The barns were in a location that gave him an excellent view of any approaching supervisors. He would sit atop the stacks of hay and read pornographic magazines. If anyone approached he would leap off the hay bales and grab a rake and shovel and pretend he had been working. He even went so far as to put water under his armpits so that it would appear that he'd worked up a good sweat. His laziness was disgusting, but it was not that quality which I cared for least. It was his cruelty.

Benedict hated animals, as had his father before him. They would never say that, but their actions yelled louder than their words.

One fine day, when Bambi the male mule deer had grown an impressive four-pointed set of antlers, Benedict decided he would enter the deer's yard. He wished to show off to an attractive college girl who was sketching the deer. During rutting season deer can be very dangerous and very unpredictable. Benedict should have locked Bambi up, but he didn't because he delighted in showing his mastery over the animal.

Benedict was carrying a leaf rake and poked Bambi in the side as he walked by. Bambi's instincts took over and he charged his antagonist. He rammed his antlers into the man's chest and knocked him down the hill. It was a steep hill, and Benedict tumbled sixty feet to the bottom. He was punctured in four places and shaken. When he stood up, the attractive college girl gave him a dirty look and walked away.

Later that day Benedict was quoted as having said, "If it's the last thing I do I'm going to kill that ———— deer!"

Nobody took him seriously, but they should have. As days went by Bambi began to lose weight. His ribs began to show and he would follow anyone who walked by his corral. The vets ordered stool samples to see if Bambi was suffering from parasites, but everything always checked out fine. We later came to believe that the stool samples delivered to us were those of a healthy axis deer next door. Blood was taken and it checked out fine. There was no good reason for the demise of Bambi.

A new keeper was assigned to work Benedict's day off. It was not long until he suspected the deer was not being fed enough to survive. In a compassionate but foolish move he dumped several scoops of herbivore pellets into Bambi's hay manger. Bambi, crazed with hunger, ate all of the pellets. They caused him to become thirsty, and he drank too much water. Bambi died as a result of the acute gastric disturbances.

The new keeper was issued a deficiency notice, and rightly so, but the real culprit went unpunished because nothing could be proven.

When Benedict and I first talked together he said jokingly, "If you don't feed them, they don't make as big a mess."

I thought he was joking, but he wasn't. All of his animals were thin and neglected. But the joke was on him. From that day until the day he was transferred, he had helpers that he knew not of. Benedict left at 4:00 P.M. and I left at 5:00 P.M. Right after he left, the senior keeper and I would slip down and give all of his animals all the food they needed to thrive—and, oh yes, to make a big mess. His new senior keeper also made him keep his corrals clean.

Six months later Benedict was fired for intentionally driving a truck into a telephone pole.

I had on occasion worked with his father and noticed he had a propensity to tease animals. He would delight in holding treats just out of the reach of the orangutans and chimps at the health center. He also would give them lit cigarettes and laugh loudly if they burned themselves.

Benedict's father was best known for having been attacked by Sam, the Bactrian camel. Sam knocked him down and grabbed his leg in his mouth. He dashed him up and down and tried to squash his head with his enormous foot. Another keeper risked his own life to save Benedict's father. He had to hit the enraged camel with a shovel and hold him off until the injured man could be dragged from the exhibit. Prior to this, many keepers had reported seeing Benedict's father offering hay to Sam. When Sam would extend his lips to get the hay, Benedict's father would grasp them with his pliers and hold him there until he chose to let him go. He, like his son, had a terrible need to dominate the wild animals. That's how they gained their identity and sense of importance.

It wasn't difficult to calculate the impact of Benedict's father's example. Benedict had learned his irreverence for life from his father.

When the Scripture teaches that the sins of the parent visit the children unto the third and fourth generation (Exod. 20:5), I take it to mean that children keep picking up the values of the parents. Providing a good example is essential to raising decent children.

One Saturday morning I was walking by the black rhino's exhibit and was angered by what I saw. There were two boys on either side of their father throwing some rocks they had collected at the rhinos. They were rather large rocks and the boys were throwing with all their might. The father wasn't saying or doing anything. He was just watching them pelt the rhinos mercilessly. I yelled at the boys to stop and they did.

"Are these your boys?" I asked the father sternly.

"Yeah," he answered defensively.

I looked at him for a moment wondering what to say next, then I asked, "If you didn't want to be responsible for them, why did you have them?"

He didn't know what to say.

"Listen, if you want to help them behave then you can see the rest of the zoo. If not, the front gate is that way. At any rate, I'm going to have security keep an eye on you."

As I walked away, I overheard him say that if they embarrassed him again he would beat them silly.

We saw a lot of cruelty at the zoo. I helped pick up marshmallows concealing razor blades and fish hooks. I asked myself what kind of tortured mind would do that? I participated in several surgeries to repair golden eagles shot by local hunters. What a waste of majestic animal. I remember grabbing a huge chunk of asphalt out of the hands of a twelve-year-old boy who was going to throw it onto an alligator. He screamed, "You can't prove I was going to throw it."

What darkness resides in a man's mind that allows these infringements and much worse? Albert Schweitzer gives us some insight in this reflection of his own childhood from his book, *Reverence for Life.*

While I was still going to the village school we had a dog with a light brown coat, named Phylax. Like many others of his kind, he could not endure a uniform, and always went for the postman. I was, therefore, commissioned to keep him in order whenever the postman came, for he was inclined to bite, and had already been guilty of the crime of attacking a policeman. I therefore used to take a switch and drive him into a corner of the yard, and keep him there till the postman had gone. What a feeling of pride it gave me to stand, like a wild beast tamer, before him while he barked and showed his teeth, and to control him with blows of the switch whenever he tried to break out of the corner! But this feeling of pride did not last. When, later in the day, we sat side by side as friends, I blamed myself for having struck him; I knew that I could keep him back from the postman if I held him by his collar and stroked him. But when the fatal hour came round again I yielded once more to the pleasurable intoxication of being a wild beast tamer!

These kinds of flaws are in all of us to some degree because of the Fall. What happened in Eden broke four relationships: man with God, man with man, man with himself, and man with nature.

For now, we must be *commanded* to be kind to animals because it's not something that comes naturally. Proverbs 12:10 shares, "A righteous man has regard for the life of his beast." Jesus tells us that He approves of the idea of helping an animal in trouble even if it means breaking the sabbath (Luke 13:15, 14:5). He sees the fall of the sparrow (Matt. 10:29). The Lord is acquainted with every bird (Ps. 50:11). Do you know how many birds there are? Billions. And yet God considers all the animals His private property (Ps. 50:10).

Animal cruelty is a terrible sin. How wonderful that the new heaven and the new earth will be free of it.

> The wolf shall dwell with the lamb,
>   and the leopard shall lie down with the kid,
> and the calf and the lion and the fatling together,
>   and a little child shall lead them.
> The cow and the bear shall feed;
>   their young shall lie down together;
>   and the lion shall eat straw like the ox.
> And the suckling child shall play on the hole of the asp,
>   and the weaned child shall put his hand on the adder's den.
>
> Isaiah 11:6–8

Isn't this great? You don't want to miss it. So be sure to be there.

Mirror, Mirror

Nobody knew why Ivan wouldn't come in to eat. His voracious appetite had pulled him through the guillotine door for twenty years of zoo life. But there he stood, just outside the door, staring through everything, into infinity. This nine-hundred-and-fifty-pound polar bear had never missed a day of eating. Food was his life. I threw him a mackerel and it landed still inside the night quarters just four feet from his face. He continued staring into space.

"Come on, Ivan. I want to go home," I pleaded.

No amount of coaxing made any difference whatsoever. I didn't have the authority to leave him outside, so I ran to get Al Franklin, my senior keeper. Al had worked with Ivan for a lot longer than I had and might have known a trick to bring him in.

Al tried all the same things that I had tried but with no more success than I had achieved.

"Did you ever drop a door on Ivan?" he asked.

"No, Al, I never have," I answered. We had a good friendship and there was no reason to believe he would doubt my word.

Al didn't have the authority to leave Ivan on exhibit overnight. So he called Ed, the principal keeper, who did have the authority. Ed's first question was, "Did anybody drop a door on Ivan?" and Al assured him that neither he nor I had done so. Ed felt that Ivan should be locked on exhibit without food till morning and hunger would be our best bet to bring him in.

Morning came all too soon and we resumed our efforts to bring in the bear. Still no success. The problem his obstinance was creating was that we could not clean his outdoor quarters unless we could lock him inside. The zoo's architect had placed the drain valve to Ivan's large swimming pool inside the exhibit with the most dangerous bear in the zoo.

Ivan was also the messiest bear in the zoo. It was summertime and by the end of the second day his pool was becoming light green with free-floating algae. The third day the algae began to settle on the sides of the pool and the exhibit began to smell musky and sulphurous.

The fourth day we tried something clever. We tied a live chicken to the bars inside his cage and let it walk about. We hoped that it would stimulate his feeding instincts, but it didn't.

We would have tranquilized him but there was a terrific chance that he would stumble into his pool and drown. Actually, there were some of us who thought that we would be willing to take that chance.

After a week had passed, you could smell Ivan's exhibit as soon as you entered the aquatics section. Every supervisor in the zoo began suggesting things we had already tried and asked whether I had dropped the door on Ivan's head. I suspected that someone had done that in the past, causing Ivan to fear going near the door for a period of time. But I couldn't think of anything I had done that might have caused this strange behavior on Ivan's part.

One week stretched into two, then three. Ivan hadn't eaten for twenty-one days, but we made sure that he had fresh water daily by directing the stream from a high pressure hose near his massive head. The weather was uncomfortably hot and Ivan was glad for a good cooling off. We had no idea how long it would be before we won the battle of wills, because fat polar bears are capable of going incredible periods of time without food if they have access to water.

On the twenty-second day, Al Franklin found me by the sea lion exhibit and asked me if I would help him. He told me he had gotten an idea that just might work. I had long since become skeptical, but I was amazed that there was a new idea to try.

Al said, "Follow me to the men's room at the chief's shack and I'll show you my idea." I couldn't begin to imagine what there could be in the men's room that might lure Ivan into his night quarters. But my curiosity was at an all-time high.

Al led me in the men's room and proudly pointed to the four-by-five-foot mirror mounted over the two porcelain washbasins. I knew I was missing something because for the life of me nothing about the mirror struck me as having the capacity for catching a nine-hundred-and-fifty-pound polar bear. I began to wonder if I was missing a philosophical approach like "the answer is inside ourselves" or something like that. Ivan was not a vain bear, and a mirror would not service his needs at all. Why, he didn't even own a comb.

"Okay, Al, I'm sure this is going to be good, but I just can't see it. How is the mirror going to help us?"

"Ivan has killed two other polar bears, right?" he said.

"Right."

"So the way I've got it figured, he hates other bears. If we prop this mirror up just behind his bars on the outside, he'll look in and think he is seeing another bear. It will make him madder than fire and he'll run in to kill it. Anyway, that's my theory."

"It's worth a try," I said, as we began unscrewing the mounts that held the mirror to the wall. We carried the mirror into the back of the bear grotto and leaned it into position so that when we opened the guillotine door Ivan would be staring at his own reflection.

Al stepped aside so that Ivan would see nothing but a bear in the dim light of the night quarters. I lifted the door and peered cautiously at our stubborn nightmare. He was instantly aroused by the bear in the mirror and moaned quietly. He rocked back and forth and then charged the bear in the mirror aggressively. As soon as he cleared the door I dropped it into place. Al had found the answer. We got a lot of good laughs because of the unorthodox nature of the capture, but everyone admired Al for his original thinking.

One of the ways man is different from the animals is that he realizes he is looking at his own reflection. He has self-realization. We may see an enemy in the mirror, but the enemy may be us. There have been times in my life when looking in the mirror was very painful because of how I was living my life. It is strange when you find yourself avoiding your own gaze because you feel that you can't respect the person you have become. Look at what James 1:21–25 has to say.

Therefore put away all filthiness and rank growth of wickedness and receive with meekness the implanted word, which is able to save your souls. But be doers of the word, and not hearers only, deceiving yourselves. For if any one is a hearer of the word and not a doer, he is like a man who observes his natural face in a mirror; for he observes himself and goes away and at once forgets what he was like. But he who looks into the perfect law, the law of liberty, and perseveres, being no hearer that forgets but a doer that acts, he shall be blessed in his doing.

Find a mirror. Look deep into your own eyes and say,

Search me, O God, and know my heart! Try me and know my thoughts! And see if there be any wicked way in me, and lead me in the way everlasting.

Psalm 139:23–24

Now do what God tells you. There is peace and joy there.

Birds and Bees

Four million, four hundred thousand different species of animals—can you imagine? That is the number of animals God spoke into existence during the fifth and sixth days of creation. That breaks down to 2,200,000 per day or roughly 91,667 species per hour, 1,528 species per minute, or 25.5 new species per second. Now, add to this the amazing fact that, with a few exceptions, He was creating males and females. It means that God was cranking out 51 different anatomies per second, each with its own behavior, unique appearance, and ecological purpose. Every species has been assigned specific and appropriate behaviors for both its sexes. Let me illustrate.

The female black widow spider is four times as large as the male, who is not black at all but white and gold. She is a deadly huntress and knows every inch of her web by feel. She is also blind. When the male comes to court her, he plucks the web at a constant rhythm which calms the throbbing black temptress. Then she quietly awaits his approach. Every few steps he plucks again so that she will not respond as if he were just any insect in her web. He repeats the process until he arrives beside her. He strokes her with his delicate front leg and begins the mating process. He is exhausted after mating and in a weakened condition usually stumbles as he attempts to leave the web. The irregular vibrations trigger her instincts to kill and he is quickly overtaken. Without emotion she adds him to her macabre pantry of stored delicacies.

Sea lion males are a study in rage and passion during breeding season. The males hit the rocky beaches and establish territories for the harems they will build when the females arrive. They fight constantly and brutally, not even taking time to eat. By the time the females arrive, the younger or weaker males have been driven off and the main bulls begin to claim and fight for as many females as they can get. The females have been pregnant for three hundred and fifty days, and they begin to give birth almost as soon as they arrive. Shortly thereafter, the males initiate a brief courtship and mating period. Then they lose interest and no longer dote over their females. Keeping their territory becomes their consuming passion. They will defend it viciously, crashing across rocks and the beach, at times crushing their mates and young to attack an invading male.

Elephants are a matriarchal society. The females call the shots. When the male elephants reach adolescence, they are driven from the main herds to form small groups of males, or they become solitary. They are only tolerated during the breeding season and then driven away again when breeding is completed.

The pied hornbill (an exotic bird with an enormous beak) finds a tree with a hollow apartment. He drives the female into it, then seals her inside with mud. She is not allowed to leave this confinement until the young are ready to leave the nest. Everything the family needs is shoved through the small opening he has left for that reason.

The rattlesnake breeding ritual is a brief erotic study. When he discovers a female during mating season, the male rises above her to full stature and sways back and forth in a captivating ballet. She responds in kind and they entwine. After mating, he crawls away (that snake in the grass!) never to see her again. She carries the young and gives birth to live babies, which are on their own from their first day in the world.

Penguins mate for life, although they spend more than half of every year separated. The Adele penguins have a ceremony. They present a rock to their beloved. If she accepts it, the pair bond is sealed and they are mated for life. It's "with this rock, I thee wed."

Wolves also mate for life. They live most of the year in small family units, forming packs only in deep winter when it is to their advantage. Because mice are hibernating and therefore unavailable as a food source, the wolves must bring down hooved animals to survive. The males love their mates and provide 50 percent of the sacrificial care of the young. They are the ideal family model.

When we come to man, we cannot discern a consistent method of male and female behavior. You see, in many relationships the male is consumed by the female's dominance and fares no better than the male black widow.

Many males consumed by their careers spend all their time building their territory. They crush their children and pursue extramarital affairs. They act like sea lions.

Some females drive off their males with unattractive fury and make it difficult for the fathers to visit children, just like the elephants do.

Some men force their women to stay home and keep them subjected, like hornbills.

Then there are those who form a partnership. They are helpmates. They work together to raise the young in a cooperative venture, like wolves. Some mate for life, like the penguins.

One of two things is true: Either man is the only species out of four million, four hundred thousand without an assigned method of relating male and female or we have a method that we are not following. What do you think?

God's Word gives us a good picture of what He had in mind in Ephesians 5:21–33.

Verse 21:   Husbands and wives are to show honor to each other.

Verses 22–24:   Wives, make your husband feel like he's important. Respect him. Treat him like he's someone special, somebody worthwhile.

Verses 25–33:   Husbands, love your wives in a sacrificial way. Serve her needs in such a way that you set her apart from all others as unique and special. Encourage her to be everything she can be. Nourish her and cherish her. Then you'll become totally united.

We don't see this kind of marriage very often. Do you think we've become too focused on who is going to meet our personal needs?

For understanding this, that in the last days there will come times of stress. For men will be lovers of self . . . .

2 Timothy 3:1–2

Good for a Laugh

I love a good laugh. It is one of God's greatest inventions. Psalm 2:4 begins, "He who sits in the heavens laughs." The following stories are offered for your enjoyment. I hope they cause you to laugh, especially if you need to laugh.

Jambie

About a year before I began my career with the zoo, a legend died. His name was Jambie. He was a large adult male orangutan. I never met the fellow, but his delightful episodes were told and retold, as all great tales should be. You see, Jambie was an incurable practical joker. His specialty was water jokes.

Over the years, Jambie learned the art of trading. He would throw food that he didn't care for out of the cage in hopes that someone would give him something he really liked. What happened most of the time was that a person would retrieve the castaway food and throw it back to Jambie. Jambie was a bit frustrated that no trade was effected, so at some point he conceived a plan to humiliate the naive zoo patrons who were missing the point.

Now it may be helpful for you to know that Jambie could hold half a gallon of water in his cavernous mouth. To entice the inept traders, he learned to drop his trading item close to the wire of his cage. When the patron would bend over the guardrail to fetch the food, Jambie would climb quickly to a position above them and spew one-half gallon of liquid all over his or her back.

He learned the art of positioning for other purposes also. He would grind up his monkey biscuits and sprinkle them just outside his cage . . . but within the reach of his monstrous hand. From the base of his palm to the tip of his fingers it measured fifteen inches. He would lay his hand down near the crumbs and wait with patience for the peacock's hen and her chicks to come close to the bait. With a sudden sweep of his hand he had new and animated toys. He would bring them into his cage and play with them for hours.

The Weekend Authority

I have listened to hundreds of zoo patrons say some incredible things about the animals, but none more incredible than what Henry told Mildred about the beisa oryx. A beisa oryx is an African antelope. It is one of the larger members of the family, standing about three and one-half feet at the shoulder. Its slender horns curve gracefully another two feet above the head. It is a combination of subtle gray, brown, black, and white—a strikingly beautiful animal.

Henry studied the oryx for several seconds. You could tell he was impressed. By the look of his clothing and the sound of his accent, my guess was that he was visiting from the Ozarks of Arkansas. I couldn't be sure, but certainly he was from somewhere in the Deep South. His voice caught my attention. I was inside a barn talking to an animal keeper about a medication he would be giving one of the animals on his string when Henry began to lecture his family on what he had learned by reading the zoo sign. I peeked out the door and saw Henry surrounded by his three little boys. They were all dressed in overalls and wore no shirts. Mildred, his wife, stood where I would have stood if my family were dressed that way in Southern California—about twenty feet away. It didn't do any good, though, because he kept shouting some new particle of information he had gleaned from a sign.

"Hey, Mildred," he hollered, "you won't believe this! This here oryx has a gestation period of 267 days. That is a mighty long time to digest your food."

"What does it mean, Daddy?" ventured one of his cherubs.

"Billy Joe, it means that what this animal eats today won't be eliminated until next February." Then he sighed and said, "Ain't that amazing?"

It was mid July.

Now You See It . . . Now You Don't . . . Now You Do!

It was clearly entered into the daily log: "Six puppies born to Mr. and Mrs. Coyote." Everybody thought they were cute. But Charlie, their keeper, found them irresistible. As soon as their mother began to take periodic rests from them, Charlie would slip in to tame them. They responded quickly to his affection.

One little female was a standout. She was gentle, affectionate, and would stay with Charlie longer than all the rest. Charlie became very attached to her and was soon locking all the others out with mom so that he could play with his little beloved. Before long, he decided that this pup was far too special to grow up in a zoo. He made the decision to take her home and slipped her out in his lunch pail.

Not too many days passed before the senior keeper noticed that there were five puppies rather than six. He approached Charlie to see if he knew what might have happened to the missing puppy. Charlie told Al that he never remembered there being six. Al must have counted one twice. Al was nobody's fool, but he decided to buy the story for a couple of reasons. First, the coyotes had no real value; and second, their future in the zoo world was very uncertain. If Charlie had swiped it, it was sure to be loved and well cared for.

Charlie lived in an apartment building with his wife, Cindy. She fell in love with the pup as soon as she saw it and agreed they should keep it. They had a sterling relationship with their landlady and she reluctantly gave them permission to care for it. They convinced her that it was simply a mongrel dog, but as the puppy grew their landlady grew skeptical. She would periodically ask, "That isn't a wolf, is it?"

"No, it's just a terrier-shepherd mix," said Charlie and Cindy.

Well, the landlady became more and more focused on determining the puppy's origin. Charlie and Cindy could see the growing concern on her face, and they knew in their hearts that they were going to have to give back the puppy or surely face the chance of getting caught for stealing. They had no friends who wanted a coyote, so Charlie decided he would return her to the zoo. He drove his car directly to her exhibit and returned the coyote pup to the cage. It was very early, and no one witnessed the glad reunion. Although she had been away nearly six months, she was well received by her family and readjusted to zoo life quite nicely.

It wasn't until Charlie's day off that anything out of the ordinary was noted. His relief keeper came to Al, the senior keeper, and said, "You have to come and see this, Al. I can't believe it."

Al followed the relief keeper to the coyote exhibit and stepped inside the cage. He was immediately approached by a tame, teenaged coyote that licked his hands and whined for attention.

"I've never seen anything like this in my life," said the dumbfounded keeper.

"Neither have I," replied Al, as he stroked his chin thoughtfully.

Al never pursued the subject with Charlie, so far as I know, but he did mention to Charlie that he'd better take a course in basic math so he could keep an accurate count of his string. Keepers speculated for months about how a coyote became tame overnight.

Give 'Em an Eyeful

Snakes have never terrified me, but the guys who worked in the reptile house were frightening. A number of us enjoyed a good practical joke, but the reptile keepers carried theirs to the very brink of impracticality.

I will not here betray all their secrets. But if by some quirk of fate the reader should someday be exposed to the possibility of being caught in their favorite ploy, I must, in good conscience, prepare them.

First, let me tell you that the guys who work reptiles are very intelligent, a breed of their own. They know their business and must maintain absolute concentration lest they make a mistake. In their arena, their first mistake could be their last. Many of the snakes are so deadly that their bites could not be survived. Unlike the rest of the keepers, the reptile keepers spent their days entirely indoors. There are no windows through which to view the sky. And walking through the seemingly endless corridors of the facility, one could easily lose track of where he is.

There are many aquariums that rest on inside shelves which are never seen by the majority of the public. They hold a variety of poisonous and nonpoisonous snakes, and some folks are forever wondering if anything has recently escaped. The color scheme, if there is a scheme, is devoid of charm. And the atmosphere is sterile, institutional, and scientific.

The reptile keepers had a great sting operation, and their favorite marks in the early days were new keepers. If you were a new keeper and they were offered the opportunity to take you on a tour, they would jump at the chance. They would begin at one end of the building, which must be about fifty yards long, and dazzle you with facts and statistics. You simply could not resist the urge to admire them for their absolute command of their subject, reptiles. You would be introduced to the world of rattlesnakes and exotic frogs and toads. You might get to hold a variety of nonpoisonous snakes, like king snakes or gopher snakes, and let me tell you, you would find yourself trusting them—the keepers, not the snakes. Well, both actually. The point was, they had you just where they wanted you by the time you were three quarters of the way through. You would do just about anything they told you to do, because you knew that what they were telling you to do was okay. It was safe.

About this time you would come to a cage. Hanging from the back of the cage was a pair of goggles, the type you would wear if you were using a table saw. They were next to a sign that immediately caught your interest. It read, "Beware of Spitting Cobra!" You would be guided skillfully into the wonderful world of cobras and their behaviors and myths. You would find yourself asking questions about the effects of the venom on your eyes and skin. You would discover that blindness may occur, along with unbelievable pain. Then in a very matter-of-fact, nothing-to-worry-about way, you would be invited to look into the spitting cobra's cage. It meant moving closer and leaning forward a little bit so that you could look over the top of the terrarium. If you hesitated, they would nonchalantly say, "No problem," or "Nothing to worry about," and then you would trust them again. While you were gazing through the screen trying to focus on the snake at the bottom of the cage, they would squeeze a rubber bulb with warm water in it. It would course through a system of tubes and gush into your eyes while they yelled, "Look out!"

There were a lot of adults who lost most of their dignity in those moments, as they said and did things we are usually spared in public life.

The laughter that echoed through that hallway bordered on the demonic, and I believe that there are many who take comfort in the fact that these men will someday stand before God on Judgment Day. They won't be holding any rubber bulbs in their hands then. No sir-ee.

Where Trouble Follows

A zoo is a terrifying place to work for the accident prone. Bill Whitecross was. In the seven years that I worked at the Los Angeles Zoo, I cannot recall seeing Bill without a bandage, cast, crutch, or some other evidence that he had been on the losing end of an untimely skirmish. Docile animals that normally adored people hurt Bill Whitecross. In fact, there was a rumor that has persisted to this day that even mealworms attacked Bill Whitecross. Now I never saw that happen, but I saw enough to convince myself that his presence should be shunned during lightning storms.

A group of us were at the white rhino barn one afternoon—for what reason I cannot remember. Sonny and Cher, our white rhinos, were pressing at the gate, hoping that someone would scratch behind their ears or around their eyes. They were very tame and could be ridden if we didn't mind arriving at their chosen destination. Rhinos go where they want to go . . . and who's to stop them?

Bill decided to step just inside the gate to accommo-date the passive giants. It turned out to be one more oppor-tunity for lightning to strike. Sonny went into instant ecstasy as Bill aggressively scratched behind his ear. Sonny closed his kindly eye and stepped forward to get even closer to the human that was showing him the kindness. Unfortunately, he stepped and stayed on Bill's foot. Now a white rhino weighs about seven thousand pounds, so Bill was experiencing the same sensation you might experience if you set a Volkswagon on your foot. He tried not to look foolish as he oooed and ahhhed, but he did not succeed. Several of us tried to push Sonny away gently. But he did not want to go, so he didn't. He just stood there on Bill's foot, waiting for more affection. Bill, however, was some-what distracted.

The rhino finally and mercifully stepped forward. Bill moaned with relief. He removed his shoe and all agreed that Bill would never need swim fins again.

Bill spent a good deal of his zoo career at the reptile house, serving as its senior keeper. Senior keepers have much less work to keep them busy than do keepers, and in Bill's case that turned against him. Looking for amusement nearly cost him his life.

Down at the very west end of the reptile house was an African python named Jeanie. Jeanie was another one of our tame animals. Bill decided that he would feed Jeanie a dead rat by hand. This had been attempted successfully on several other occasions, but never by Bill. Bill waited until a group of zoo patrons was in front of her massive cage and then he dangled the tempting morsel in front of her mo-tionless eyes. He must have had a fleeting glimpse that her eyes were clouded over because she was going to shed. He may have had just enough time to think that this may not have been the best time to feed her because she couldn't see the rat clearly. Jeanie, by the way, was fourteen feet long and about twenty inches around. Well, Jeanie was never one to turn down an hors d'oeuvre, and she launched forth. She missed the rat by five inches, but—you guessed it—she grabbed Bill. Her nostrils were aglow with the smell of a rat, and from her perspective, she had grabbed a giant one. She yanked Bill into the cage and quickly threw two coils around the surprised senior keeper. His efforts to extricate himself were absolutely futile, and the terrified zoo patrons sensed they were watching a life-and-death drama. Bill was too embarrassed to call for help and continued to struggle with the adamant python. One of the patrons ran around the building beating on doors until an angry keeper near the other end of the building came out to investigate. The hysterical patron finally conveyed the emergency and three men ran to the aid of their supervisor. He was freed from the coils of the python, but he was never able to escape the retelling of this story.

Cockatoo, Cockatoo

If you ever visit the zoo's Australian section, be sure to stop by the cockatoo exhibit for a while. They are beautiful, entertaining, and some of them even talk. They have often been people's pets before coming to the zoo, and about half of their owners named them Cookie. This is easy to determine because most of the previously owned birds say, "Hello, Cookie."

Mark Gentry enjoyed the ability of being able to impersonate the cockatoos' voices. One could not tell which was the bird and which was Mark. Mark was their keeper. He would often hear patrons attempting to strike up conversations with the cockatoos that talked, and one afternoon he had a bright idea. He stationed himself in the shrubbery next to the exhibit and waited for some enthusiastic visitors to respond to the cockatoos' endless chatter. If a patron repeated one of the bird's phrases, Mark was set up for several minutes of a Candid Camera-type encounter without a camera.

"Hello, Cookie," offered a bird.

"Hello, Cookie," answered a patron.

"What's your name?" entered Mark, but you couldn't tell it was Mark because he sounded just like the cockatoos.

"My name is Barbara," answered a rather attractive patron. Then she would add, "What's yours?"

"Cookie, silly. You just said 'Hello, Cookie,' so I thought you knew," said Mark. Barbara still thought she was talking to a bird. She usually caught on when one of the birds said, "So, Barbara, what's your telephone number?"

One day a rather loud, critical, overfed, and unattractive lady brought her little tiny husband to the zoo. Perhaps you might form an accurate mental picture if I simply told you that on that day we could account for the whereabouts of at least one of Cinderella's stepsisters. Her face was adorned with a permanent frown and her demeanor suggested that she was just daring something good to happen so she could step on it. Her husband just stood there, "Yes, darling"-ed her as she berated the zoo, its animals, the zoo food, and him.

Mark was in the bushes and one of the cockatoos said, "Hello, Cookie."

The lady stared at the bird for a second and responded with, "Hello, Cookie, yourself."

In the twinkling of an eye, Mark responded with, "Hi ya, Fatso."

She gave the closest cockatoo a stare that would have frozen the Medusa, then she clobbered her husband with her purse and said, "Henry, let's get out of here." She stormed off fully convinced that she had been insulted by a bird.

Life truly is a zoo.

CHRISTIAN HERALD
People Making A Difference

Christian Herald is a family of dedicated, Christ-centered ministries that reaches out to deprived children in need, and to homeless men who are lost in alcoholism and drug addiction. Christian Herald also offers the finest in family and evangelical literature through its book clubs and publishes a popular, dynamic magazine for today's Christians.

Our Ministries

Family Bookshelf and **Christian Bookshelf** provide a wide selection of inspirational reading and Christian literature written by best-selling authors. All books are recommended by an Advisory Board of distinguished writers and editors.

Christian Herald magazine is contemporary, a dynamic publication that addresses the vital concerns of today's Christian. Each monthly issue contains a sharing of true personal stories written by people who have found in Christ the strength to make a difference in the world around them.

Christian Herald Children. The door of God's grace opens wide to give impoverished youngsters a breath of fresh air, away from the evils of the streets. Every summer, hundreds of youngsters are welcomed at the Christian Herald Mont Lawn Camp located in the Poconos at Bushkill, Pennsylvania. Year-round assistance is also provided, including teen programs, tutoring in reading and writing, family counseling, career guidance and college scholarship programs.

The Bowery Mission. Located in New York City, the Bowery Mission offers hope and Gospel strength to the downtrodden and homeless. Here, the men of Skid Row are fed, clothed, ministered to. Many voluntarily enter a 6-month discipleship program of spiritual guidance, nutrition therapy and Bible study.

Our Father's House. Located in rural Pennsylvania, Our Father's House is a discipleship and job training center. Alcoholics and drug addicts are given an opportunity to recover, away from the temptations of city streets.

Christian Herald ministries, founded in 1878, are supported by the voluntary contributions of individuals and by legacies and bequests. Contributions are tax deductible. Checks should be made out to Christian Herald Children, The Bowery Mission, or to Christian Herald Association.

Administrative Office: 40 Overlook Drive, Chappaqua, New York 10514
Telephone: (914) 769-9000

Fully-accredited Member
of the Evangelical Council
for Financial Accountability